"In this extraordinary, hy
poetic journey – Szirtes r
childhood in Europe's da
Hungarian uprising. He brilliantly captures how sometimes it's those closest to us who remain the most mysterious"

PATRICK MCGUINNESS, author of *Other People's Countries: A Journey into Memory*

"Knowledge is partly invention, Szirtes says, memory is mostly invention, and 'the trick is to invent the truth'. It may be a trick but it's one he pulls off brilliantly in this compelling memoir"

BLAKE MORRISON, *Guardian*

"A book full of warmth, grief, curiosity, wisdom, staggering anecdotes and a coming to terms with the vicissitudes of 20th-century history . . . [a] highly original telling of the author's mother's life and the heartrending events through which she lived"

CHARLIE CONNELLY, *New European*

"A truly remarkable book about identity, image and memory. It is fiercely compelling"

EDMUND DE WAAL, author of *The Hare with Amber Eyes*

"Unforgettably sad . . . Szirtes has made [his mother's] monument. It is a courageous and remarkable achievement. I've read no memoir that moved me more" MIRANDA SEYMOUR, *Financial Times*

"Exceptional . . . There is much more to this scrupulously written memoir than I have been able to convey. There are photographs throughout the text, but those in the final pages are heartbreaking"

PAUL BAILEY, *Literary Review*

"Szirtes uses his poet's eye to build images and details that bring his mother superbly to life . . . [this] is a beautifully written and utterly compelling narrative" IAN CRITCHLEY, *Sunday Times*

"In this quest to understand the enigma of his mother's life and death, George Szirtes travels back from personal memory to deeper history, as he reconstructs his family's tragedy-darkened past . . . An original, probingly thoughtful memoir whose restraint only increases its poignancy and impact"

EVA HOFFMAN, author of *Lost in Translation: A Life in a New Language*

"[An] exquisitely told memoir . . . By telling the story of his mother's life backwards Szirtes has performed a sort of conjuring trick . . . Not simply a memoir but a hybrid of history and biography interspersed with photographs, poems and several standout moments"

ANNE SEBBA, *Spectator*

"As isolated snapshots build into a family portrait, and a historical fresco, we grasp the wider picture . . . beautiful, devastating"

BOYD TONKIN, *Arts Desk*

"Like a film in reverse, this narrative structure not only reclaims a time of innocence and hope but also functions as a form of healing, an undoing of her pain" FIONA CAPP, *Sydney Morning Herald*

"Magda Szirtes is intense, untameable, tantalising and compelling. George Szirtes is tender and astute in trying to understand her, percipient in analysing the enduring fragments of her life – letters, tape-recordings, photographs, memories – yet ever-aware of how little it is possible to know. The result is engrossing and profoundly moving" KEIRON PIM, author of *Jumpin' Jack Flash*

"He works, frame by frame, through a sequence of ever-older photographs, employing her own chosen medium to interrogate the mystery of her existence, and the fallibility of memory"

ARIANE BANKS, *Tablet*

WINNER OF THE JAMES TAIT BLACK MEMORIAL PRIZE
SHORTLISTED FOR THE PEN ACKERLEY PRIZE · SHORTLISTED FOR THE JEWISH WINGATE PRIZE · SHORTLISTED FOR THE SLIGHTLY FOXED BEST FIRST BIOGRAPHY PRIZE

George Szirtes

THE PHOTOGRAPHER AT SIXTEEN

The Death and Life of a Fighter

MACLEHOSE PRESS
QUERCUS · LONDON

First published in Great Britain in 2019
This paperback edition published in 2020 by

MacLehose Press
An imprint of Quercus Publishing Ltd
Carmelite House
50 Victoria Embankment
London EC4Y 0DZ

An Hachette UK company

A CIP catalogue record for this book is available from the British Library.

ISBN (PB) 978 0 85705 855 3
ISBN (Ebook) 978 0 85705 852 2

10 9 8 7 6 5 4 3 2

Designed and typeset in Quadraat by Libanus Press, Marlborough
Printed and bound in Great Britain by Clays Ltd, Elcograf S.p.A.

THE DIVER

There is a passage in Anthony Hecht's long poem "The Venetian Vespers" in which he imagines the process of constructing a life backwards. He sees it as rewinding a film where

> . . . people make their way by jigs and spasms,
> Impetuous leapings, violent semaphores,
> Side-slipping, drunk discontinuities,
> Like the staggered, tossed career of butterflies.

At the end of the passage he imagines a diver emerging feet first from the pool.

> But best of all are the magically dry legs
> Emerging from a sudden crater of water
> That closes itself like a healed wound
> To plate-glass polish as the diver slides
> Upwards, attaining with careless arrogance
> His unsought footing on the highest board.

Moving backwards may be like healing a wound, returning to a perfect unwounded beginning where all is innocence and potential. There is innocence in a photograph too. The faces that look out at us are ignorant of what is to come. None of this, as they say, was meant to happen. It is only we, we gods of time and space, who know their future.

ONE

The Last House

1

The ambulance was waiting at the junction. She had taken an overdose and time was short. The driver thought he saw a gap, moved forward, then stopped because the gap wasn't big enough. The car behind ran into the back of the ambulance. The ambulance was damaged. Drivers got out and my mother died.

It had been the hottest summer for many years and the news came the day before we were to take a short holiday in Wales. It was July 31, 1975. Clarissa's parents knocked at the door to tell us she had died. We had no telephone then so they had to walk down from their house on the hill. Having consoled us, they left. I didn't quite know how I felt about it. Very soon afterwards the local Anglican vicar came round on a chance call. We invited him in and had a conversation as normal. After about ten minutes I said: Excuse me. My mother has just died. So he too left.

Why did we have no telephone? There wasn't the money. We had no car either. I was teaching at a school three days a week. All we had was the house – rented from Clarissa's parents – each other, and our son, Tom, who was just one and a half. Clarissa was four months pregnant with our daughter, Helen. My mother had always wanted a girl child and now, as it was to turn out, she was going to miss one.

I had to let our holiday landlady know that we could not come. I must have gone down to the nearest telephone booth – where was it? – to explain. She was understanding.

The blankness I felt was tinged with guilt. If I don't feel anything at one moment am I capable of feeling something at another? At all? I knew nothing then of her past, of anything that had happened to her and all she had survived. Nor did I know much about my father and his close brushes with death. I had no sense of them as heroes or powers or even as people in their own right. They were my parents. They did not speak. I did not ask. What was it I was supposed to feel, after all. For whom? For her? For me?

2

In February 1975 she had been called into hospital for cardiac catheterisation to investigate the infection she developed a year before. She had to have it in two stages. She writes from hospital having completed one stage, fearing the next, the letter deeply concerned about our son's measles (which she spells "measels").

Here is a late photograph taken in her dream kitchen towards the end of her life. Here a suicide note found among my father's papers. It was not the last attempt or the last note, just one of a series. Her death came later.

She was capable of leaving strong, indelible marks. Shortly before she died she made a tape on our old family Grundig in which she sang us happy birthday for the future. Not once but several times, once for each birthday, until her voice gave out. My father passed me the tape after she died. I still have it, but have only played it twice in forty years. I needed to hear her voice on those occasions because I had forgotten it and to assure myself that she had actually made such a tape.

There is an old joke my father told us about the balance of

power between husbands and wives. Two men in a pub. Who makes the decisions in your house, asks one. I make the big decisions, my wife the small ones, the other replies. Give me an example of a small decision, asks the first. A small decision is like, should I buy that hat, that coat, do we wallpaper or paint, do we buy this house or that, do we go here or there on holiday, do we live in this country or that country. All minor decisions, says the man. So what is a big decision, asks his friend. Should Red China be admitted to the United Nations, the other replies.

That was a long time ago. She made both the big and small decisions and he would agree that she was right.

It was she who had made the decision to leave Hungary in 1956. It was she who decided what my brother and I should be in life. I was to be a doctor or a professor, he a solo violinist. They were reasonable things for her children to be, but we both failed her. I did not get into medical school and my brother had to be content with being an orchestral violinist. She always wished the very best for us. I knew that, and my brother probably knew it.

She had even decided who my father was to marry after her death – an Iranian doctor. He didn't. Maybe he should have. He married a Hungarian instead, a woman very unlike my mother.

3

The doctor was called Hashmat and looked like a fleshier version of my by now much thinner mother, with the same dark, sculpted hair, the same natural poise and the same fierce, hungry look in her eyes. My mother's preference was for exotics, for the startling, the smart, the genuine, for those with hearts relatively close to their sleeves, and Hashmat must have ticked all those boxes. What is more, at about fifty she would have been roughly of an age with my mother. We met her once, but I had no idea then what she had been groomed for.

Did Hashmat really know it? Had she accepted the role of the second Mrs Szirtes? And if so, how was she persuaded, in the course of what manner of conversation? My mother was capable of conversations like that. She was an expert if somewhat obsessive operator of the spirit. She might well have said something like: "Hashmat, I am dying or I'm going to die soon and I can't leave my husband to fend for himself. You need a husband [I presume Hashmat will have had one and either divorced him or that he left her, or that he might have died, which might well have provided an occasion to touch on the subject] and mine is ideal; understanding, hard-working, solid and decent, with an interesting history." She might have sold him like that, as a car with one careful owner.

It can't have been like that, can it? But by what act of empathy could such an arrangement be made?

The story of "the arrangement" came from him, after she died. He had, he said, agreed with her plan – to keep her happy – but had no intention of complying. Did Hashmat? Would she have been disappointed he did not keep his end of the bargain? Or was she too playing along? Seeing the photograph of her now, she looks like the typical, modern, secular, well-educated Middle Eastern woman we then assumed all well-educated Middle Eastern people to be. Surely the whole world was going to become ever more modern as it went along. Nothing could stop that, could it?

Would religion – or indeed culture – have mattered at all? Not to him. The secretary he was to marry two years later was not Jewish but Protestant. He himself, after all, was a Jewish atheist, a thorough, if non-militant, unbeliever.

Where did my mother find Hashmat? On what byway of her recent life? It might have been at one of the hospitals she stayed at for operations, observations or convalescence. I would not have known. The previous six years of my life had been spent away from her, first at art school in Leeds, then in another part of London, then in Hertfordshire. My parents were where I left them, in North Wembley. Parents are generally where you leave them.

4

It was I who took the 1974 photograph we have of Hashmat. She is at one side and my mother at the other. My mother is a shock. She seems to have her left arm missing, but it is simply tucked away behind her. My father's arm is around her as if to prop her up. She has all but wasted away. She is wearing a wig full of curls that only draws attention to her frailty. She is gazing with

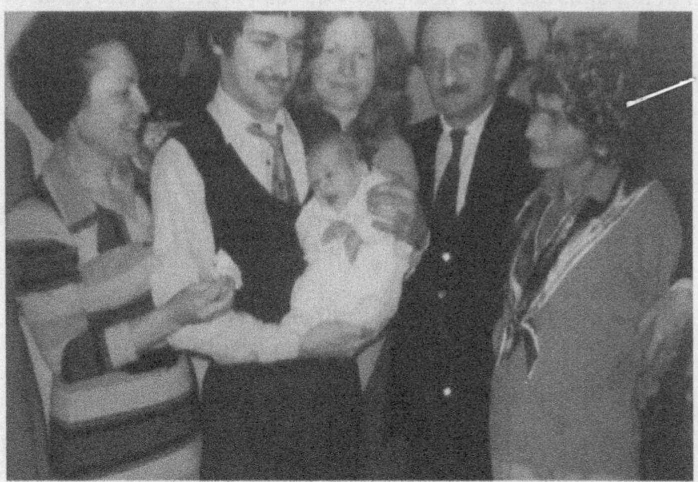

solicitous intensity at the baby, our son Tom, at the centre of the picture. Her smile is from somewhere beyond the flesh.

Beside the five adults – Hashmat, my brother Andrew, Clarissa, my father and my mother – there is someone else in the picture who hasn't quite got into the frame, a woman in a grey dress. We can't see her face, there is only a faint suggestion of hair. I do not remember who it is – I can't even think who it might be, unless it is Sharon, the wife of the American naval officer who lived next door. Sharon and Ezzie were my mother's kind of people.

There is a later photograph of her, just one, showing her without the wig. She is holding a slightly older Tom. Her natural hair is silvery-black, dense, and clearly dry. The face remains wraith-thin.

5

Photographs are skin. Sometimes the skin is healthy and fresh, at other times it is hardly there. Old skin is cracked and creased: what it hides it also reveals. Beneath the skin, the flesh; under the flesh the bones and the working of the organs. We guess the organs from the skin. Dead skin falls or floats away from us, is everywhere around us becoming dust. The rest remains. We crawl into it and make some kind of home in it. Haven't you got a home to go to, people ask us. Skin is home.

I take a photograph from the album. There is a wardrobe and a chest of drawers. The drawers are closed. What is inside the drawers? Could I strain every nerve and recall the contents? I doubt it, yet something about the room, its position in time, its location in life, seems tantalisingly present.

But the photograph is not the presence, it is only the skin of presence, a presence that is so like flesh that I could press my nose into it. It has a scent.

A life reconstructed from photographs is all skin and scent. Somewhere within are bones and organs, an operating system like any body, however wasted or, as with the baby – our son – practically new.

6

By the time the kitchen photograph was taken she was a wreck and knew it. It was she, of course, who decided we should buy the house. The kitchen had been the most treasured item in it. How she longed for it! Heartbreakingly for her we were gazumped not once but twice before the sale went through. The kitchen had a black, neatly speckled lino floor, wood-panelled walls, the fixed furniture tops were clad in curdled-white formica while the drawers and cupboard doors were covered in a peel-and-stick-on light-grey gingham vinyl that, by the end, had begun to peel off. The whole room felt sticky to me.

It sticks to her too. She is trapped in it. She is the remnant of the startlingly attractive woman she had been. Her hair is lacquered and piled high. She sits behind the table holding a small, dark-green coffee cup. An ashtray lies in front of it. She is on Consulates ("cool as a mountain stream") by this time. A red soda syphon is perched on a narrow shelf to her left. Behind her, above the fridge, an orange Le Creuset pan hangs on the panelled wall. It looks isolated and too heavy.

Displacement hits you later than you expect, just when you think you have settled down and become part of the world all over again. That is when it begins to ache, when a certain inarticulable desolation creeps in. Your body is not where your body ought to be: it shouldn't be behind that table, between those wooden panels, with those gingham drawers and that Le Creuset pan. It is as if you had ghosted in but left your soul behind.

What lay beyond the window? There was a flat, featureless lawn with a border at the end of which stood a sideways-on garage (the one in which I was prepared to spend the night when she locked me out because I was late home, though she came out after half an hour and let me in). To the right, the back door opened onto a small greenhouse in which she tried to grow tomatoes. She had not much strength left by then, but she wanted life around her, just as she had in previous years when she had surrounded herself with caged birds – zebra finches, crossbills, lovebirds, budgies, canaries – and, before them, with domestic fowl, ducks and geese that left the garden a swamp crawling with slugs.

Before that there was the sparrow, Csuri, that had fallen out of its nest and which she nursed and domesticated so it would flutter around the room and land on our heads or shoulders when we called it. When my father came home from work the sparrow would fly to him. We could even take Csuri shopping, but one evening when it landed on the floor she stepped on it by mistake. She was devastated. She wanted life, but she wanted it nurturable, captive and devoted.

7

She died shortly after I had finished my second year of teaching. The first had been a three-day-a-week part-time post at a co-ed comprehensive in Cheshunt that was some two hours' travel away, and while I liked the school and the teachers I worked with in the art department, the four hours of travel was too much, so, in the next year, I took on another part-time post teaching English in one of the two girls' schools in Hitchin, not the one that had been a grammar school until recently but the secondary modern. At the end of the school year I left that one too. As far as my mother was concerned that would have been two failures. Not that she said as much – she had grown used to disappointments – but her ambitions for me were always grander than my own. My only ambition – still recent – was to be a poet, and while I had published one or two poems in significant places, a book seemed far away. Teaching was a job, not a career. Art school instead of medical school or university certainly counted as failure. Working artists were rare and who, after all, made any money from poetry, especially someone unlikely to write whole books. My only success was in marrying someone she immediately loved.

She must have believed her hopes for her children to be realisable. If nothing else she willed them into reality. She had accomplished a great deal through sheer willpower, almost everything in fact. I, naturally, respected her will, but was no longer prepared to bend to it. Poetry saved me from the consciousness of being someone else's failure. If I failed at poetry it would be unbearable, but at least the failure would be my own. I did not think I would fail. How could I think that and go on?

8

Her surgeon was the best there could be. Magdi Yacoub was the world's leading expert on heart transplants. She spoke fondly of him. She was to have her mitral valve repaired. Now that I myself am due for a by-pass her procedure is becoming real to me, but hers was forty years ago. Everything would have been longer, harder and more risky.

I see her in two different hospital beds at different times. The first is on an ordinary ward, presumably before the operation, the second is in a private room, clean, white, with a window opening onto a large garden. It is a small room, but quiet. When we visit her, two of us sit, the third stands. The next time we visit she is in the garden, beginning her convalescence. We are there with her, my father, brother, Clarissa and I. Two nuthatches are hopping around the bushes nearby. They are bold enough to come close. My brother identifies them for me. They are pretty little things, blue and yellow with a gorgeous streak of black, like extended eye-liner, running from tip of beak through to the neck. Andrew has developed an interest in ornithology and I am learning from him if only by testing him from books, covering up names, and pointing to pictures of birds that he must identify. He also has to describe the call and habitat. This habitat is Harefield Hospital. It is late spring or early summer. The time is confused, two occasions separated by years but telescoped into one.

Mitral valve surgery involves cutting through the sternum to get to the heart. It means carving through bone and flesh. You are temporarily a carcass. They stop your heart and connect you to a machine, they pick, prod, and fiddle with you. Then they reconnect you, swab you, and pin and screw you back together. It takes weeks to get over it if you are strong and if it is successful. The first operation was never going to be the whole answer, they told her. She would have to come back for a second in due course. Having told her that, they instructed her to rest but she wouldn't because she couldn't. She wasn't made for passivity. That made it worse the second time, in 1973.

This time there was an infection. What they tell you now is to have a dental check beforehand so that infection should not enter through the gums. Did they then? Were they even her own teeth by that time? I never saw her without them, but then I wouldn't, nor would she ever let us see. My father's teeth were not real. Dentures changed the shape of his mouth in subtle ways. Her mouth looked slightly different in later photographs, but I may be imagining that.

9

One forgets faces but remembers photographs if only because they stand still and never change. They fade, of course, but even so they make a home in memory and settle in like cuckoos, ousting live images, the tiny mental film clips that appear to constitute all we recall of reality. But film clips are no more natural than photographs. The truth is I have forgotten her face, in the sense that I am no longer sure whether what I imagine as alive and in motion is not simply a psychological mechanism whereby any photograph is a frozen moment with life flowing on before and after it. In other words, I don't know whether it is my personal memory or an impersonal response that animates her for me. That does not mean her face has disappeared, only that it has become a series of images, a zoetrope, a notional weight attached to weightlessness.

After she died, I decided to distract my father by getting him to talk about their life. He was devastated and said he remembered nothing, but then I asked him about his childhood bedroom and he began to talk. We went on talking week after week for more than two years, at which point he remarried and our conversations became rarer and more difficult to arrange. Not impossible, just rarer.

I have a great deal of my father's voice on tape, but of hers I have only the crazy birthday messages. Not having listened to them for many years, at this distance I expect her voice to be deep. I expect it to be a little hoarse, slightly cracked and tired. That goes with the images I have, the late, frail images that seem to have eaten her, that have themselves been consumed.

10

Her friendships had been leaking away. Illness and exhaustion brought out a latent bitterness in her. She did not want to see people. She did not want to be seen. Travelling took too much out of her.

She fell out with people. There were what she considered to be betrayals, betrayals having run through her life, some deep and genuine, some possibly imagined. It was not that others fell out with her – it was always she with them. I am sure now that she was aware of this, that it was part of the despair and fury that drove her on to the end.

All her life she had been marvellous at making friends. She had been beautiful, energetic, direct, warm and passionate; quite irresistible, it seemed, so even I, as a resentful adolescent, could see that. My father faded into a rational, second-string, quite undeserved ordinariness next to her. People loved and admired her: she had more than presence, she had history, a heroic history. Sometimes it almost seemed as though we were expected to be extensions of her. I once said as much to my father as I was getting ready to go out. She was standing next to me and had made a comment I no longer remember. It was the only time I recall him hitting me (she had hit me as a child, he never had). It wasn't a hard or painful blow, but it was surprising. His heart wasn't in it, but his sense of justice was roused. How dare a son of hers question her selflessness?

He was right to be angry. I was not entirely wrong, but I was crude. And cruel. Not quite in control of myself.

That was before I left home. We did not see her very often after that, only on holidays.

11

She often talked of voluntary euthanasia, of how desirable it was, how good it would be to be in control of one's death, how it would put an end to everybody's suffering, not just one's own, but everyone else's. This conversation generally took place around the dinner table, not so much a conversation as a monologue followed by protests and silence and resentment. Our adolescent resentment. What right had she to talk like that, to consider her own life first, especially when our own were yet to be decided, not by her but by ourselves? Did she not realise how selfish she was?

How dreadful we were, I now think. How selfish and ignorant. But that is now. Everything is different in retrospect. This too will be retrospect in time.

Over the years I have changed my mind about euthanasia, but that might be for equally selfish reasons. Now that I am nearer death myself, now that it is emerging as a shape, I think it would be good to set the conditions for it. In any case I have now seen what dying can do as it grows attenuated, wrapped in care, time, and other people's sapped energy. All the awkwardness it entails. I would like to spare them that but chiefly, of course, I would like to spare myself the consciousness of the whole hideous process.

There was no such process for her, or if it existed it was compressed into a few years in her late forties. The sinking was fast, whirlpool fast, and in the end she did go down, though the actual way it happened was something of a botch.

12

In my first year as an art student in Leeds I attended a séance at my digs. It was my one and only séance. Some eight or nine of us gathered round a table in a darkened upstairs room. We set the letters of the alphabet out in a circle, took a wine glass and began asking questions of a notional spirit. The glass began to move. Do you have messages for us, spirit? asked our medium. One of us was addressed by an Uncle Charlie he could not remember. It warned him to avoid death on the coming Bonfire Night (a number of us took it upon ourselves to act as his guardians that night and no harm came to him). I was the only person to receive a less than sinister message: "Live in peace. *Selah*" the glass spelled out. It could have been fixed, of course, but who in that company would have been familiar with the ending *Selah*? I myself had not heard it before. It was, I discovered afterwards, from the Psalms and signified a musical rest, a kind of pause.

No-one in my family, as far as I knew, had lived in peace, not for long at any rate. We had all pitched up in one place or another as a result of war or other seismic affairs. I myself had only arrived at the séance table by way of a revolution some thirteen years before. It was assuring to be wished peace.

What would my mother have made of this dabbling in the murk? Had she ever done such a thing? There was a great deal lost in the murk for her. One of my earliest Hungarian memories was of seeing a film with her. The film concerned a superstitious woman. I can see the woman now, knocking nervously at a door and climbing the stairs to consult a fortune teller in a darkened room. She was the dupe: the "gypsy" fortune teller, the confidence trickster. It was a comedy. We were sitting near the end of a row of hard seats. My mother held my hand. The mystery that was no mystery lay behind the door, up the stairs.

There is something here that suggests the idea of breath, peace, darkness and mystery. They belonged together in her, in that voice on the tape that even now I find hard to listen to.

13

Towards the end of her second stay in hospital she made friends with a Caribbean-born nurse who was a Seventh Day Adventist. For the first time in her life she was tempted by religion. Born into a secular Jewish family in 1924, as we now know, she had little enough to do with religion apart from a few gestural formalities.

She claimed to be Lutheran, or that is what my brother and I were always led to believe. It wasn't true, but we didn't know that as children. We had never stepped inside a synagogue, never kept any Jewish holidays or customs: we were not even circumcised. Whatever the truth, her experiences during the war confirmed her as an atheist.

Seventh Day Adventists keep the Saturday sabbath and believe in an imminent Second Coming. Between death and that Second Coming, they believe, the soul simply goes to sleep while the world undergoes a period of investigative judgment whereby salvation or damnation is determined as in an infinitely long judicial enquiry. Believers, in the meantime, receive a heavenly sanctuary that began in 1844 when the hope of the Second Coming ended in the Great Disappointment.

What of this appealed to her is hard to say. I suspect it was less the doctrine than the radiant benevolence and happiness she detected in the nurse. She had been much moved by what she had heard of gospel choirs and adored Mahalia Jackson. Jackson and Paul Robeson were twin gods. She felt that the natural, apparently boundless joy of the singing was a release from the manners and hypocrisies of the societies she knew. They signified freedom of the soul.

It was the same freedom she perceived in gypsies. She would go and play with gypsies in her childhood and later, even as an adult, took great pleasure in dressing as a gypsy, with shawl and headscarf and full, wide skirt. Her dark complexion and black hair was in character for it. Both she and my father enjoyed listening to gypsy bands and recordings of gypsy songs. They both knew a good many by heart. The music moved her to tears and made her dance. She particularly loved dancing to the *csárdás*. I saw her do so in my childhood. The romantic idea of Romany life was fully alive in her.

She was not alone in this. Hungarian society in the mid-twentieth century was united in its love of traditional gypsy music. You could hear it daily on state radio. It was a condition of the soul. The Irish scholar Walter Starkie set out on the Hungarian gypsy road with his fiddle in the Thirties and recounted his highly coloured adventures in the book of his travels, *Raggle Taggle*. The soul, as apprehended by him, was wild, sensuous and freewheeling. My mother would not have disagreed.

A good many Hungarians now regard the emotional appeal of the words as grossly sentimental and the music itself as a set of fancy clichés mercifully scrubbed away by Bartók and Kodály. But it was a valid state of soul then. The unfettered exhilaration of the gospel choir, the radiant joy of the Seventh Day Adventist nurse, and the romanticised gypsy condition must have touched the same nerve in her.

14

The house I left, the house in which she took her own life, was an end-of-terrace property in a quiet suburb of London populated by the upper levels of the skilled working class and a few middle managers. Being an end-house meant there was more room for the garden she longed to cultivate. It was built between the wars with fake timbering, somewhere between Arts and Crafts cottage and what Osbert Lancaster termed "Stockbroker Tudor". The dream kitchen lay at the back of the house down the hall. There had originally been two rooms downstairs, but they had been knocked into one sometime before we moved in. There is a photograph of the frontage taken after her death with my father leaning against the recessed porch. The windows are the same upstairs and down, both have six panes with a faintly Palladian arch in the middle. Not that these architectural terms would have meant much to them when they bought it, but the whole is different from next door with its plain oblong windows. The oriel window of the small bedroom where my brother and I slept in a bunk bed is visible on the right. The whole has a touch of modest but satisfied ambition and is certainly larger than either of our two previous houses. It is a station in life.

My alienation from the house was probably due to my age. The furniture was G-plan mostly, comprised of a round, glass-topped coffee table, a low sideboard, a brown three-piece suite and moss-green walls on which hung a few reproduction paintings by Moses Soyer. She would have chosen them, as well as the light-brown fitted carpet and the curtains with their large abstract patterns. It was clean and uncluttered apart from the piano, on top of which lay a pile of sheet music for her children to play since neither she nor my father had ever taken music lessons. Some bric-a-brac of the period was tastefully distributed on the sideboard and the corner table, including a couple of black bent-metal stick figures influenced by Picasso, one with an African headdress and earrings. The Soyers hinted at an acceptable form of Expressionism fading into general twentieth-century modern, along the lines of Bernard Buffet. (I was growing sophisticated and contemptuous of such things.) The dining table was at the other end, facing the back garden, as was the television and a wood-burning stove. The dining table was used for the family games on Sundays, for rummy or whist, or bridge or Monopoly. Guests ate at it: as a family we used the smaller fold-out table in the kitchen.

This too was a state of soul, clean, very carefully maintained. It was decoration but with a light continental touch, non-aggressive, subtle, unpretentious, what she would call in Hungarian slang *guszti*, meaning chic or in good taste. She was the ultimate authority on *guszti*.

The staircase was the place where a few less favoured decorative pieces might be displayed, including gifts from friends. When she fell out with them these objects vanished. This included a piece of geometrical macramé by one woman whose friendship had lasted several years. I hated it. My wounded but unvoiced snobbism was at its most intense then.

Upstairs there were three rooms and a bathroom. The box room was the one with the bunk beds. My parents' bedroom came with a long, white built-in wardrobe running the length of one wall. Everything could be hidden in it. The double bed with its twin bedside tables faced it.

The street, being a cul-de-sac, was quiet. The quiet of north London suburbs is generally decorous and a little oppressive. Children did not play in the street. There was no revving of motorbikes or engines. No-one came home drunk and screaming, no smashing of bottles late at night. We wandered through streets, alleys and passageways named after the Romantic poets. The main road was a street away with a playing field beyond. I never saw any games played on it. The underground station and the nearest bus stop were some ten minutes' walk away. It wasn't like anywhere she would have lived before.

The other, bigger, upstairs room had been furnished as a study for us, the boys. I can see it now. A built-in cupboard, a wardrobe, a chest of drawers, a settee, two sets of wall-shelves containing very few books – there is a *Reader's Digest Encyclopaedic Dictionary*, a James Bond novel, an anthology of Hungarian verse, and a copy of Bill Naughton's *Alfie*. There is a polished formica-topped writing desk with some of my school books on it. My brother's music stand and his violin case rest in front of a set of golf clubs. None of us had played golf except of the miniature kind at the seaside, but swinging a club in the open air was a way of exercising my brother's violin-playing shoulders and expanding his chest. The game was thought appropriate for him because, unlike me, he was physically well balanced and co-ordinated. For me there is a microscope that was always more promise than achievement and there, on the floor (yes, this is another photograph) is a Grundig reel-to-reel tape recorder, the very instrument on which she was to record that last terrifying set of happy birthdays. From here it looks like an image of desolation. Then it just felt like it.

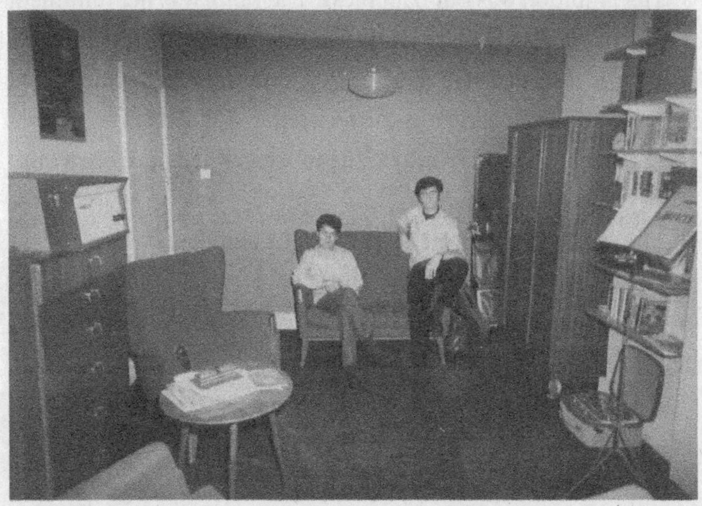

I say desolation, but the room was only my particular corner of the whole. The desolation lies in my memory of it, memories of my wasted hours of revision, redeemed only by the small, sly notebooks in which I had begun to write poems, at least one a day, partly as a simple attempt to be anywhere but here, but also – more fortunately – as a form of fascinated distraction by words that had nothing to do with obligation. Two years later, the poet Martin Bell, my first real but completely unofficial mentor, was to tell me that poetry was, at heart, a secret and subversive pleasure. This was the room in which he was first proved right.

My condition was dwarfed by my brother's. It was the room in which he practised the violin for four, five, six hours a day, after school. It was where he wrapped himself around demanding pieces and exercises of increasing complexity to fulfil his obligation to become a solo violinist. He continued to do this after I left home. His life was that room, that violin, that space filled with ambition, the ambition chiefly hers.

Her ambition was our happiness. The violin was her fulfilment of that happiness for him. It got him far further than the microscope got me, since he did go to Trinity College of Music and carved out a long career as an orchestral violinist. Even so that was not what she had in mind. The room was meant to open onto more glittering vistas.

She pursued the future with a jealous and demanding energy. She listened intently to my brother's hours of practice. She especially listened out for his gaps of rest, to his slacking. He had been granted a God-given talent by a non-existent jealous God, a God who demanded utter devotion and despised the half-hearted, a God who spat out the lukewarm but took the fully striving to the burning fires of his or her heaving chest.

It is her desperation I am describing, not her selfishness. She had suffered history, now history had to redeem itself through the future, a future of which, she had realised, she would not be granted more than a glimpse.

15

Given their backgrounds it was not surprising that my parents should be natural Labour voters. They referred to Sir Alec Douglas-Home as "Old Death's Head". Harold Wilson's calm pipe-smoking, steady-eyed socialism was far more to their taste.

They had seen a great deal of instability in their lives and were politically attuned to trouble. My father had been not just a member of the party in Hungary, but a leader of a department in the Ministry of Construction. His views on industrial relations were those he brought with him to this country. British industrial relations, he felt, were class-ridden and archaic. Why should management dine in one canteen, the workers in another? He identified naturally with the workers. My mother was probably to the left of him in her egalitarianism. Both of them, like so many others in Eastern Europe, had been radicalised by the war.

But they had had enough of violent change. The late Sixties concerned them and the Seventies were to shake them up even further.

It was moral decline they feared in the Sixties. They had grown up with the conservatism of the orthodox left, not with the anarchic drop-outism and drug culture of the hippies. That, of course, was another reason why my choice of art college seemed such a dangerous choice to them. Long hair horrified my father. Even my mother was repelled by it. It was a rip in the fabric of life.

Their fear of moral and social decline was exacerbated by what they saw as Britain's industrial disintegration. They had grown up in a world in which the label MADE IN ENGLAND was a guarantee of quality, a world in which Britain produced cars, steel, coal and textiles and had a formidable fishing fleet as well as a mighty, world-famous navy. It was not that they took pride in these things as such, it was simply that, for the first time in their lives, they felt as reassured by them as by that spread of pink across the world map. It was a haven. Like many survivors of the war in Eastern Europe they admired Churchill. In their mind's eyes the war had been won by Stalin, Churchill and some Americans. Churchill had stood up to Hitler.

Now Churchill was dead. Harold Wilson devalued the pound in 1967. That was a blow. There was inflation. Industrial relations became ever more unstable. What did they think was happening? My grammar school became a comprehensive in 1967 so, for the first time in seven years, my brother and I were in the same school – not that I saw much of him there since we were still on split sites. I cannot think they would have been displeased by that.

The Grosvenor Square demonstrations against the Vietnam War in March and the May 1968 events in Paris would have shocked them. They were not alone in being shocked, of course, but in the context of the history they knew and had experienced it was different. The Tory victory of 1970 would not have been their victory, but the three years that followed – the years between my mother's first operation and her second – will have had a profound effect on their lurch to the centre right.

Whether they felt whatever they felt as a couple or whether they responded as individuals is hard to say. We didn't notice any difference because by 1970 the political was being ever more heavily overshadowed by the personal issue of her health and state of mind but, going by my father's evidence on the tapes, he was the pragmatist, she the potentially explosive ideologue. My father would have had a ready understanding of *realpolitik* in all its forms: my mother thought in terms of justice and fairness. She could be quite absolute about this and was not above lecturing my father, though with ever less energy as time went by.

The loss of energy was not a matter of gradual and steady decline, but of exhaustion punctuated by explosions. My father was the most frequent object of her rages, which would be sudden and without apparent cause. She would shout and scream and occasionally hit him, then be abjectly sorry and write him the most loving notes of apology. I wondered at my father's calm and patience. Love, I half understood, could be like this, and especially fierce, abiding love. We, as almost grown children, understood that notes had been written. Later we saw one or two. My father's explanation of her outbursts, according to my brother, was that they occurred just before a minor heart attack. But surely the minor heart attack – whatever that was – had been brought on by the outburst. That, of course, left the outburst unexplained.

The oil crisis of 1973 and the subsequent three-day week coincided with her second operation. The photograph with Hashmat in it would have been taken then, in those circumstances. My parents had signed on to Bupa's private health insurance scheme. Having begun life in England reading *News Chronicle*, they had moved on to the *Daily Herald*, followed by the pre-Murdoch *Sun*. After Murdoch they shifted between various newspapers, but by the time my father remarried in 1977 the *Daily Mail* had become, and remained, their regular paper.

16

The sacredness of family Sundays was not to be questioned by anyone outside the family. Others could be brought in but we could not opt out. So, in the second half of the Sixties, when my first long-term girlfriend, Julia, steadfastly refused invitations to join us for whist or rummy or bridge and demanded that I spend that time with her instead, she became my mother's enemy. My loyalty to the family cause – I think my father would gladly have let me go – was in serious doubt. Once tensions had risen they could not easily be resolved. Even the idea of some Sundays at home and some away was an offence to my mother. I could go out during the week and on Saturday and even stay out relatively late, but not on Sundays.

It was not only Julia who kept me out late in the week but also the friends I made once I had started writing poetry. Like me they were secret poets trapped in the wrong subjects. The three of us tended to meet at Stephen's, in his room in the family flat in Burnt Oak, and we brought with us whatever new or old poetry we happened to discover in second-hand bookshops or the school library. That could be anything from the Beats by way of Rilke, Donne, Adrian Henri, Baudelaire, Rimbaud (delicious, dangerous Rimbaud!) and Thomas Lovell Beddoes, whose *Death's Jest Book* seemed the most romantic of themes.

> Old Adam, the carrion crow,
> The old crow of Cairo;
> He sat in the shower, and let it flow
> Under his tail and over his crest;
> And through every feather
> Leak'd the winter weather . . .

Beddoes was everything we were not but had intimations of being. At seventeen and eighteen we were natural seekers and melodramatists. It was when I was returning from one of these late-night meetings that my mother locked me out but quickly took pity on me.

She and Julia locked each other out. There was one occasion when Julia and I briefly split up and I went out with someone else. It was just once. Shortly after, the girl rang me at home and the telephone was picked up by my mother. Having found out who she was and why she was calling, she immediately encouraged her to take me away from the dreadful Julia. I am trying, the girl replied, a story she repeated to me sometime later. In any case the relationship with Julia was soon, if temporarily, repaired so nothing came of the brief interlude.

It was not the first time my mother had tried to manipulate my relationships. A couple of years earlier I had gone out with the daughter of one of her friends. She was a very bright student and my mother had encouraged me to ask her out. But the night before our first date my mother drew me aside to tell me that the girl did not like being touched and that it might be best if I were careful and did not take her out again. I had no idea what she was up to, but she effectively sabotaged the date. Sometime during the evening at the cinema I had an intense feeling that the whole thing was my mother's affair, not mine, and that she was sitting beside us. Maybe this was really a date between her and her friend, my date's mother.

17

She was enormously relieved when I brought Clarissa, my wife-to-be, home for the first time in 1969. My father immediately fell in love with her and with the yellow dress she was wearing at the time.

It was the yellow dress my father fell
in love with, skimpy in late Sixties style.

My father usually works till six. Meanwhile
the garden waits. The kitchen. The terrible
last years in the last house in the last street [. . .]

He thinks you beautiful as she once was
but gentler somehow as if you'd come to mend
his life or mine. And she is sitting at the table
where light is dancing as it always is.

The poem has my mother sitting at the table as in that last kitchen photograph. She too fell in love and discovered, to her enormous relief, the kind of person she always needed to confide in (confiding in people was the core of her trust). This girl was not going to take her son away. She would not shut herself – or her son – off from family.

So all proceeded well. My mother would take Clarissa aside and confide in her. She came to our baptism by full immersion and wrote to tell her friend how amused she was when we emerged from the water "like two drowned rats". It was a joke for her, but a good one. She had sought to hide her own, and therefore her children's Jewishness from them, and this was a brilliant stroke of good fortune. Now I, as a baptised Christian, would be even more likely to be preserved from what she had gone through.

Naturally enough she was delighted when we decided to get married in 1970. She had already got to know – and was welcomed by – Clarissa's free-thinking Baptist parents, and the marriage represented yet another vital step away from the minefield of Jewish identity. Now her son would be safe and, Judaism being a matrilineal religion, her potential grandchildren would be even safer.

For the wedding she wore an elegant black dress and made herself at home among my wife's more distant relatives and those kind members of the congregation who had helped to organise the reception. She looks an exotic creature in the wedding photographs, like a film star walking a sober street. She sways with sensuality and holds the photographs together. It was a summer wedding and, compared to her own wedding in 1946, quite large, though very small by normal English standards.

Knowing we had no money and that all we had arranged was a cut-price week in a distant cottage on the Isle of Man, she suggested, or rather insisted, that she, my father and my brother be our hosts for a week in Switzerland after we returned. She had my father reserve a different hotel for us and made it clear that we were not obliged to spend our free days with them, though we probably would. It was fine. She was discreet. She did not intrude or dominate. She did not enquire as to the success or otherwise of our first two weeks of marriage. She was simply determined that it should work.

The hovercraft ride on the way home was a ride of terror for many. We rose and fell back into the wild waves that threw us high into the air so we could drop again. There was screaming and vomiting.

Later, we were enthusiastically invited to stay a few weeks with them in the last house. Still being students and having nowhere else in mind at the time we accepted. We stayed in what had been "the boys' room". She would come in for a chat some mornings, while we were still in bed. The talk was of ordinary things. Maybe she just wanted to see us together and be assured of the reality of the marriage. Clarissa did not mind. She thought it was odd but she was not fazed by it even if I was. During the day we were in the streets, in another part of London, giving out leaflets, ironically enough for an employment agency, the only summer job we could find that year.

The question of madness – whatever constitutes madness in this spectrum of behaviour – would arise now and then after her death. Maybe the house was an asylum of sorts and that was why I distanced myself from it. But what constituted madness in a world that had at times seemed determined to produce it? Maybe the whole idea of madness was nonsense and it was sacrilege even to think of it! The fact was she had suffered before and was certainly suffering now.

> Let us drink then, my raven of Cairo!
> Is that the wind dying? O no;
> It's only two devils, that blow
> Through a murderer's bones, to and fro,
> In the ghosts' moonshine.

And what if it were all moonshine?

18

Was it my madness or hers, or simply a common form of desperation? Might suburbia have exacerbated it or even produced that desperation in her?

I doubt that it helped. Being trapped in it, in a house at the end of one of its terraces, will have been a factor. It was not I who was really trapped there – I was going to be leaving sooner or later, I was only impatient – it was she. She had always been a working woman. She needed work not so much for the money as in her earlier life, but because her energy and dignity demanded it. She was not cut out to be a housewife, especially not an invalid housewife. She had to be out and about, believing in what she was doing and doing it as intensely and as meticulously as she could.

She had been hospitalised three years before, in 1967, and been ordered to rest. The housework could be done by an agency and the costs would be paid by the council. This was a temporary arrangement, only while she was bed-bound. The cleaners came during the day and I met only two of them on my early return from school. Both were male. One was an out-of-work young actor who was to commit suicide a year or so later. The other was a singer called David Jones with eyes of different colours. He was later known as David Bowie. I bumped into him one day when he was cleaning our box room, he had picked up one of my poetry notebooks and was reading a page or two. I did not feel it was an intrusion. It was rather flattering that he should want to. We went downstairs and talked in the kitchen. He was taking lessons in mime and was releasing, or had released, an album under a different name. He seemed impossibly glamorous, his life a succession of brave, exciting acts I could only imagine. It could never happen in this house, in a suburb like this.

Nothing could happen in life here, which is why it had to happen in the imagination. I had only imagination. My mother had experience. Living in such a house in such a suburb would have been quite different for her. Suicide and imagined glamour passed through the bones of the house. Like the actor, Thomas Lovell Beddoes had committed suicide: his poetry was as glamorous in its own way as the singer was in his. The deathly glittering image of Beddoes was a desired intimation of life beyond the house for me. For my mother, life and death was what she brought into it.

After I left home I never wanted to live in a suburb ever again. To imagine suburban life as a goal seemed almost a death wish. Did she want to die in a place such as this? Surely not! She was only fifty-one at the end, and it must have been apparent to her by then that this was a mistake, literally a cul-de-sac. Might that explain the despair of the dream kitchen photograph? And if it does, does it mean that dream kitchens stuck in their period inevitably speak of death, or at least whisper of it? Or is it just that all photographs do that?

There is a courtyard in Budapest, at 10 Magyar utca, in the inner city district, with which I fell in love some thirty years ago, so much in love I knew immediately I wanted to die there. Why there? Because the courtyard spoke to me in some way. In its age, condition and dimensions, in the level of its noise, its delicacy and wear, in the texture of its walls and the unevenness of the old glass in its inner windows, in the way two or three pigeons flapped lazily across it, in the way it led from a quiet street by a quiet square into a main street roaring with noise and yet was sheltered from it, it summed up something I both recognised and desired.

There must have been something like that for her, a place where she might have been content for someone to pronounce the words: "Look thy last." That house, in that street, in that suburb cannot have been it. Perhaps it was the house of which she had spoken, the one in Transylvania, from the windows of which she, as a sick child, could look out onto the park and see her school friends skating on the frozen pond. I am only imagining that, of course, but because I myself have looked for it and seen a likely candidate for the spot, I can see her there, in the same way as she might have been able to see herself later. But she could have seen herself in many other places. There are places people go that others can never see.

19

There was a house before the last one but I have little memory of it. She was still working at home some of the time. There was the light-box on the table, a set of photographic oils, some tiny sable brushes and some slivers of razor for scratching out unwanted marks.

> When she bent over the light-box her face shone
> As though she herself had been the source of light,
> A moon to a diffuse rectangular sun . . .

The light-box was an old prop. I remembered the one she used in Budapest, watching her work, seeing the slightly sinister under-lighting of her face, the face defamiliarised then settling back into its known configuration.

Sometimes she was hand-colouring, sometimes simply re-touching. When retouching, the coils of film looped over the side of the light-box and

. . . flopped in tight
Orthodox curls over the edge of it
And her hair too fell forward, black as night.

Both retouching and hand-colouring were common practice at the time, but the golden age of hand-colouring was over by 1940, the year she started learning photography.

Hand-colouring was as skilled an art as embalming, everything life-like yet more perfect, more as one would wish to be, or wish to be seen, whether by oneself or by one's family. There is always an ideal face behind the real one but what she looked to discover was something other than the ideal: it was the alternative model of self as display. The smoothness, the image of health, the mortified charm, the glow of the cheeks and the light in the eyes, could be conjured and applied from a point cultivated in the imagination. It could not be applied to a real face, of course, only to the image of a face on a sheet of photographic paper, as one image superimposed upon another. The truths of photography are provisional, but what truth is not?

Hand-colouring, it was a form of art,
And when you bent over your work I saw
How art could not obey a natural law,
That faces flowered and that teeth shone pale
As distant neon: memory would fail
To keep the living and the dead apart . . .

She hand-coloured photographs of us. We too were being prepared according to some model of perfection. But this is not a poem, this is her working away, growing tired, occasionally grumpy, sometimes flying into a rage, then carefully bending over the box, as she would over me or my brother.

20

It must have been at about the same time, when the illness was biting into her, that she began to attack images of herself and occasionally of me and my brother. She did not attack all the images, only the more recent ones. She would take one of the retouching razor blades and scratch out her face or ours, or if there wasn't a blade handy she would work it over in fierce black biro. We never saw her doing this but came across the photographs later.

The sheer fury of her effacements was shocking. There is perhaps something demonic about the face, any face, at times. What looks out meets what looks in: the exchange is as much exorcism as execution. It is not so much recognition as the fear of recognition. Or, worse still, the fear of unfamiliarity, the fear that the image has lost all contact with the self. Maybe she was attacking that demon, the demon she recognised.

We work our way back through history through a forest of wiped faces. Some scraps of cloth, a found button, a cap, the sole of a shoe, a coin. A ghost crew. Bones in mass graves.

21

The house before last hardly exists. If I crawl back in time I enter a fog at this point. Even the photographs of the interior of the house dwell in half-light and I am not entirely sure whether they were taken of the previous house or this one. The wallpaper looks faintly familiar and accompanies us as we grow and pass from eleven to sixteen. But I cannot believe we were there for five years! How can five entire years vanish into such dense fog? Let me recall what I can.

The furniture is the first detail to emerge from the fog. It is definitely cheaper than the furniture in the final house. The whole place is more cramped and dark and fugitive and yet, I suspect, it is actually happier. My mother is younger. She looks chic, almost playful. The fog has cleared a little but much is still lost. Where, after all, is the house? I have an address but when I look on Google Street View it is not where I expect it to be. It is further down the road, not at the corner as I imagined. Where there must have been a garden there is instead a concreted drive with cars. But it's the wrong house. The address is misleading. No. 1 – our address – does not come at the beginning, rather in the middle of the street. This was the kind of inconsistency my parents found disorientating in England. They had read about the choking English fog, the London pea-souper. We had walked down streets on days when the next lamp-post was invisible until you bumped into it. Where were the street names? Why did street names change, apparently arbitrarily, from one corner to the next? Why were houses numbered in idiosyncratic ways? Why did some houses have no number but a name? Here we were in no. 1, slap bang in the middle of nowhere, plonked in the middle of a street. Why?

If she was still going out to work when we moved in, she was certainly not working by the time we moved out. Her condition was becoming ever more acute and this was the place where the operations started. We moved there to avoid steep hills such as the one we lived on before, hills that were hard to climb and left her breathless. It was not far from the last house, but the terrain was flatter, broader, edge-of-industrial, threadbare yet – just about – desirable residence territory, for some at least, for certain classes, classes that, presumably, included us if only in economic terms. But those terms were something after all! As my father later said: Imagine that, in the country only five (or six, or seven, or ten) years and we have this! A house with a front and back garden, a car, a television, summer holidays . . .

Well, yes, summer holidays. There she is on a beach, possibly at Paignton or Weston-super-Mare in a one-piece swimsuit, her hair sculpted into something helmet-like, stiff, French and chic. Her waist is slim. Now I see that she is perfectly proportioned. I missed that at the time. She is grinning and holding a cigarette in her hand. The next photograph might be at Sandown. Now we're at Chertsey. Now in Dorset. Then in Wales. There is Dunkery Beacon and there we are on top of it. We lie out on beaches, on deckchairs, on inflatable beds. We pose by cliffs, by Guinness Clocks, by matronly seaside landladies who fall for her as dizzily as a younger man might. Now we pose by a Hillman Minx now by an Austin or Morris 1100, now a Ford Cortina, a company car, and now by an automatic model we were offered after my father smashed his ankle and hip falling from the first floor of a construction site. I remember his face in hospital then. It was green with pain.

But here she is again, her hair free this time, with my brother and I. Photographs keep track of her. Her hair keeps changing. First the long black gypsy locks, then piled into a beehive, then cut into a tight elegant cap, then sculpted again, this way and that. Here she is posing on another beach, the pose natural, her body swaying a little, not too much. Her swimsuits remain one-piece, never low cut, never what she would have regarded as vulgar. She brandishes her children like trophies or hangs on to them as if smitten by unexpected anxiety. Photographs show how she dresses them up in dazzling white. She trims their hair into crew cuts. She moulds them the way she moulds herself. Her confidence seems endless.

My father is stoical as ever. He looks steadily ahead, a picture of let's-be-sensible, must-keep-the-ship-afloat calm. He is calm as we venture abroad into the Swiss mountains and snake up narrow roads. At one point the rear wheel of the coach hangs over a dizzying precipice. She gives a low cry, but she doesn't panic. He whispers reassurance. Later she sings and dances. She talks to everyone. She has so much life that we feel drained of it. We seem to be living on her terms. But we are becoming adolescents. Maybe that is why it is all a whirl, maybe that is why our lives seem so decentred, so not ours.

22

Nothing of this would have been possible in Hungary. No seaside, no car, no weeks of summer holiday. But then, one year, in 1968, the year I was about to leave home, the year after our move into the last house, we decided to visit our home country for the first time. My father still had family there: she did not – she doesn't have any anywhere, or so she assumes by now, having searched hard enough – but she did have dear friends.

She is more than ambivalent about the place; she is hostile and angry. She has her reasons which are deeply lodged and are not to be shifted. My father shares some of her feeling, but in his typically quiet undramatic way. That is why, at odd times, for curious reasons, we accepted invitations to the Romanian Embassy in London for film shows and exhibitions. I don't know how they came to her. The events were semi-formal, slightly stiff affairs that relaxed into conversation for her. She would watch the film, pick up a book, nibble some of the petit fours and find people to talk to though we never met them afterwards. We had never been to the Hungarian Embassy and I know of no invitations to attend anything there. She was, of course, born in Romania but into a Hungarian family, and Hungarian families in Romania tended, for historical reasons, to be, if anything, more patriotically Hungarian even than Hungarian Hungarians. Under the circumstances this fond attachment seemed particularly odd. These were deep waters to us children and we wouldn't have known what or how to ask, although we did note that our father did not accompany us to Romanian events. We returned from such events with books and minor treats. But what was she getting out of it? Was she really interested in Romania? She must have been. But why?

At that time Romania had a new leader called Nicolae Ceauşescu. He had only been in power since 1965 and was regarded as a comparatively liberal figure. What is more he did not break diplomatic relations with Israel after the Six Day War of 1967. All this would have counted for her, but it will not have been all. The reasons must lie deeper.

23

It is 1968 now. I am nineteen. We drive to Hungary, stopping in Germany and Austria. The taverns are boisterous, all tankards and singing. In one hotel there is a dance. An older man, his face jagged with clear, sharp folds of skin, asks my mother to dance. There is something demonic about him. He leads her an energetic dance once, then does so again. My father sits out the two, but eventually gets up and tells the old man that her heart is weak. The old man does not believe him. He insists. From where I am sitting I think she would like to go on, but I sense that the old man is a bully of some sort. He is dangerous. He is the emblem of a past we don't talk about. Her dancing on is a way of challenging him. Her way would always be to challenge. But my father is right, she shouldn't be doing this. She is forty-four, still very handsome and shapely. But she has already had one operation.

It is August and Budapest is very hot. It's best not to go out in the afternoon, especially for her. Heat saps her and makes it hard for her to breathe, so we spend most days in the flat of dear old friends. The man was my father's employer just before and after the war. The woman, his wife, clearly loves my mother and my mother loves both her and the husband back. The couple have moved into the flat of the woman's elderly brother who lives in the same block. We are to stay for three weeks with some excursions.

I hear the language around me, a language I have hardly spoken for almost twelve years. It is a tingling sensation. For her it is a return not just to familiar words but to a familiar self. Budapest still looks like a war-torn city. Buildings are damaged, there are vacant blocks like missing teeth, people are scared of the police, but something about the height, width, length and depth of things is so familiar it leaves me off balance. We see my parents' old friends. We meet members of my father's family. His own mother and sister are no longer in Budapest but in Buenos Aires, having left at the same time we did, but he has a couple of cousins. One of the cousins' sons is our age and is on military leave, having a party, so we go along and try to converse in Hungarian. Who is Marcuse, one asks me. Marcuse is a name I have heard but I have only the faintest notion of his ideas. It doesn't matter, we are exotica and, as things stand, Hungary is going through a liberalising period. It is all a little heady.

We drive down to Lake Balaton, where everyone goes to cool off. Cousin Pista and his wife Cili come with us. They sit with my parents by the lake and talk or play cards and, when it grows dark, buy some *halászlé* – fish soup with hot paprika to taste – and eat it with the sweat pouring down their backs. One evening at an inn my mother offers me a piece of bread dipped in a particularly hot *halászlé*, warning me to be careful. It almost blows my head off. She laughs and carries on eating.

She seems happy enough in a country she has talked of hating. She doesn't trust it an inch, but she is with friends and is becoming fully part of the place: the lake, the food, the friends and the little dacha where we spend our Balaton days. I lose track of her a little because a group of boys and girls about my own age have adopted my brother and me, and one of the girls has become fond of me. She asks me what I do, and I tell her about doing sciences and that I might be reading psychology at university or possibly going to art college. But what I really want to do is write poetry, I say. She asks me to read one of my poems. I have one of my little notebooks with me so I do. She seems impressed. We kiss. We promise to write. She does so in a beautiful, controlled hand. Then we go back to Budapest.

It is a hot, stifling night and I wake early, at about 5 a.m. I go into the main room and quietly put on the radio. It's the news. The Hungarian army, along with the Russians, the Poles and the rest have marched into Czechoslovakia to put down Dubček and the Prague Spring. They do not call it the Prague Spring, they say "reactionary counter-revolutionary forces". It is the morning of August 21. Constitution Day. St Stephen's Day. Fireworks Day. We are ten days into our three weeks. When my parents wake up I tell them the news and they are immediately concerned. I am nineteen and could be called up. We have British citizenship by now but have not got around to renouncing Hungarian citizenship. Anything could happen. So we get out that same day by the only open cross-border road and drive home.

I don't remember the return journey, but it will not have helped my mother's heart. She distrusted the city and now the sudden, unexpected happy time was over. I am sure the visit was good. It was like touching a source of vibrant energy for her. Budapest was a valid place. She was fully herself, fully with old friends who had known her for years. She was replete with the taste and sound of something that echoed her own sense of being. She will have recognised something of herself, as even I did of myself, though my recognition was uncertain. We drove back to London, to the new house that was still new and had not yet closed about her.

And who was it who did not join in the invasion? It was the Romanians! They refused, the only member of the Warsaw Pact that dared to do so. In fact, they condemned it. Not only did they maintain relations with Israel, but they established diplomatic relations with West Germany. This was her Romania. It was also Ceauşescu's, but she was not to see what became of him.

24

The scene in the tavern, or what I think of now, a little melodramatically, as dancing with the devil, was partly a challenge to all she knew – and she knew a lot – of the demonic and oppressive, partly a flirting with it. There had always been, as far back as I can remember, a flirtatious streak in her. She would pick up on any suggestive element in a conversation and push it further, as if daring both the other person and herself. Nevertheless, my father told me later, she was rather prudish in terms of nudity. Lights had to be off. She was both shy and bold.

Early on in our time in England we were good friends with a fellow refugee family who lived close to our first house. The family consisted of a man and wife and their two pretty daughters, who were just about our age. He was a photographer and she, so it was hinted, modelled glamour shots for him. I have a separate memory of overhearing the woman talking to my mother on a beach. She was wondering whether my mother would pose too. They were comparing their breasts. I don't imagine anything came of it. I was no more than nine or ten at the time. She would have been happy enough to talk about it, but I doubt she would have done it.

Later on in a boarding house – on one of those summer holidays – she holds forth on the subject of strippers, her talk swaggering and brash, as though it were the most normal thing in the world to be talking like this to a man she does not know. The man opposite leans forward and tries to keep up with her, but he can't. She doesn't bother about my presence. I think she may even be trying to impress me.

There is a studio picture of her sitting on a table, her legs drawn up next to her, looking cool and sophisticated. It is a fairly standard model pose. A bikini-clad girl might sit on the bonnet of a car at a motor show like that, but my mother is not in a bikini. She is quietly dressed. She exudes self-conscious control. She knows what she is doing. She is playing a part that is in her range, for which she has a certain flair. She may be thirty-eight or forty.

How tall was she? About 5′1″. My father's intimate name for her was Csöpi, meaning Shorty or Titch; hers for him was Mackó, meaning Bruin or Teddy Bear. Both were a little below average height in Hungary for the period. Both were slender. Both were striking-looking, my father on account of his big gentle eyes and hooked nose, she on account of her dark hair, fine lips and animated look. I doubt he ever regarded himself as handsome: it was my misfortune to look like him, he said. She, on the other hand, knew she was beautiful: it was my brother's good fortune to look like her. On one occasion – it is recorded among the photographs – she dressed my brother as a girl, in a skirt and a headscarf. He is far too young to mind and performs a little dance for the camera.

25

We are gradually retreating in time. I gaze at the photographs of the period, particularly at those of the second house and try to make sense of them. It is quite different from the last; less modernist, more cramped, more thrown together. It is also darker, or rather the photographs suggest something poorly lit. That wallpaper was chosen from specimen catalogues. It consists of faint grey vertical reed-like trickles or columns of winding flowers. There is a red armchair and a blue sofa both slightly angular. There is a fireplace with a glazed pearl-grey ceramic surround and another in dark brown, but there is a plug-in electric convector heater in front of it. At least the shelves of small ornaments look the same. More bent-metal figures. A coolie pulling a container for two tiny bottles of wine, both empty. A tiny amphora. Two small pots of cacti. On the mantelpiece there is a reproduction of a well-known popular painting by Gyula Derkovits from the era of Stalinist Hungary and, next to it, another reproduction of a yawning man by Rembrandt.

Everything is as neat as can be given the economic circumstances. We are neat. In this photograph she stands in the centre in blue trousers and a mustard-coloured top revealing a shirt and a cravat. She has her best smile on. We, the boys, are each side of her, both in pastel-blue cardigans, with white shirts and blue ties. I am taller than she is now, awkward in black National Health glasses, clearly introspective. My brother has not yet had his growth spurt, he pulls a startled face, a joke grimace.

We dress up for photographs, or rather, are dressed up for them. Everything here is posed. Now I am in front of the window in my smart suede jacket, now we are with my father by the Trixette record player, now in front of the D.E.R.-rented television with a slightly incongruous red toaster on the formica-topped sideboard.

None of this is ideal; the ideal is to come, because there must necessarily be an ideal. For now she is in a dark-blue dress with a necklace of large glass beads in matching blue next to my father, who is smart in a white jumper. We, the men, wear ties. The performance demands it. We are not allowed to be scruffy or louche. I am, by now, the most likely to be scruffy, but not in photographs, some of which are, I am certain, to be sent to friends still in Hungary, or to family in Australia.

We have family in Argentina too, my father's mother and sister and the sister's growing family, but they are the great unmentionables. They don't exist. My father should not even be writing to them. If my mother knew he was writing she would throw a fit. The paternal side is forbidden territory, unforgivable. No doubt he does write, but it must be in secret. When we receive a small seasonal gift from Buenos Aires she immediately throws it away. Later, after she dies, my father re-establishes the connection with his mother and sister and visits them two or three times. That must be how we come to possess photographs of them from that period. They could not have sent them at the time unless they sent them to his workplace. And where would he have hidden them? And why all this secrecy and hatred? We don't yet know. That lies further back.

Meanwhile this: the forbidden connection, the secret correspondence, the secrets generally. We seem to be born out of secrets. But isn't everybody?

I am constantly surprised by how beautiful she was. I never noticed it at the time.

Photographs are moments of noticing. They are isolated acts, usually of awareness on the part of both photographer and photographed. It is a moment's contract. The space between photographer and photographed is sacred space. Others must not, will not, walk across it. There is preparation involved: dressing up, combing of hair, adjusting make-up, a choice of prop and backdrop, of angle, of shadow, of depth of field, of contrast.

The time between old photographs shrinks. Soon there is nothing but photograph.

26

Registering her is the project, and manic control, at this stage of her life, is the theme. Does the photographer control events through selection? How far does control approximate to care? My mother's choice of subsequent partner for her shortly-to-be-widowed husband is one extreme aspect of her sense of care. She knows my father more intimately than anyone else. What she understands is that he needs a wife, that he is not, by nature, an independent being. She fears that he, the kindest and most warm-hearted of men – as others including my in-laws noted – might make the wrong choice, that he might be miserable with the wrong woman. (She turns out to be right.) And there are so many wrong women out there, she thinks. She is under no illusion about that.

But what if he marries a woman who steals her children's inheritance? The children were always number one. He accepted it. The children, or rather her intense love, hopes and understanding of her children, was the point. My father, she believes, is weak enough to let another woman take advantage of him. He does not have the moral fibre to resist it. Most men don't, she thinks. She is under no illusion about that either.

Something must be done to prevent that happening. The children must be protected and the best way to protect them is through her equal share of the house. She thinks she can safeguard us by handing it over to us, her children, so that we might exercise control. It leaves our father helpless, of course. He can't sell half a house without his children's permission. On her death he lets us know that it is we who are in control of the estate and asks us to return our half of the house to him, which we do. It is more than embarrassing, it is shameful that we should proceed on the assumption that our father would sell us short, and indeed, when it comes to it, he does not.

What does it say about their marriage, their entire relationship? That she was the dominant partner? That he was as weak as she assumed? But he never seemed a weak man to us.

In the photographs of them together we are aware of a proud melancholy in my father. He prepares himself to be a subject, for his subjection, then pulls himself together and faces the camera. He hasn't given up agency in his life, or where he has chosen to yield it. It was his decision to do so. There is one of him in the 1960s, in a zoo, and somehow on the other side of a wire fence so he looks like one of the animals on display. He wears – deliberately? – a hangdog look. It may be ironic, it may be posed on the whim of the photographer, my mother. Try to look like one of those melancholy beasts, she might have said. It would be so funny! And it is. But it is he who assumes the pose. He interprets his position behind the fence as a joke he might make against himself. After all, my father was not a weak man. Starting from nothing as a child he achieved two major successes of his working life, once in Hungary and then again, starting from nothing once more, in England. He believed his greatest gift was for management. He could think his way around a problem and solve it. He could direct the gifts and energies of others to everyone's advantage. This was his way of directing his own gifts at home.

Women are the stronger sex, he told me once. Once upon a time this was romance. Perhaps it still is when the Will is made. Perhaps romance is all it is.

27

The first house was small, a terrace with a small front and larger back garden in a cul-de-sac in a north-western suburb of London. It marked the beginning of our acclimatisation to English life. Though the house was small, as were the rooms in it, it was still the most space we had ever had. There were three bedrooms after all. It was in a decent working-class area, close to my new primary school and to streets with far bigger houses that were divided into luxurious flats. The only problem was that it was near the top of a steep hill. Shops and public transport were at the bottom, on the main road. Leaving the house was easy: returning to it was hard work without a car and we didn't have one.

It was particularly hard for my mother. She had found employment in Oxford Street at a photographic studio, working in the laboratory in the cellar where the air was poor and light was bad. She wanted to work, she always had.

The hill was a mistake my father ever after regretted. It was the hill that ruined her heart, he said. But he would not have made the decision about buying. Her desire was always pitted against his reason, and though reason occasionally won out, it did not in matters like this. I remember her coming home, how we would sometimes go to meet her and how she would have to keep stopping, struggling for breath. Although she changed jobs later and found work in the local main road the house was still at the top of the hill she had to climb.

How did we manage to buy a house at all? The prologue to it was a flat in Hendon in a street that no longer exists, the M1 having been built across it. The house had been next to the railway line to Cricklewood. We knew it was temporary, and it had to be, because it was cold and unhygienic. It consisted of two rooms with two single beds in each, the larger room with a table, some chairs, a wardrobe and a curtained-off sink and electric cooker, none of which I remember. The bathroom was up the stairs, attached to rooms occupied by a Scottish family.

The refugee committee paid for it until my father received his first salary, he having found employment with a plumbing, heating and ventilation firm in Woburn Square which meant a tube ride to Euston. The rent was ten shillings a week, my father remembered. He had a good head for figures. This was about March 1957. I was making very rapid progress with my own English in the nearby primary school, but we were in ever more urgent need of better accommodation. We played by the tube line. One night a wasp stung me in the ear. The place was damp.

The refugee committee could not help, but they suggested that the British Council might because they had some properties in Croydon and were prepared to give refugees loans to put down a deposit. Croydon seemed very far away. Nevertheless my father went to the British Council who gave him an application form to fill in. Another committee would consider the loan. After two weeks we learned that they had approved it. So we bought the house on the hill which was not in Croydon. It was a proud day. Surely it would mark the beginning of a happy period in our lives.

After a few months we rented the television from D.E.R. and took photographs of ourselves in front of it. My mother's hair is still youthfully long and black. Her cheekbones are pronounced but far from gaunt. Her elbow is propped on the television table which is covered with a patterned cloth. The room is small. The

curtains are floral, as is the wallpaper pattern under the picture rail. There was also a floral settee. The decor is rudimentary, neither her taste nor his. It is what was available. But she is beyond all this, beyond the modest suburbs of north-west London, beyond even the television which is on to show it is actually working. The television was vital. It was England in English in our own back room.

I wrote about the photograph much later in a poem filled with retrospect.

A PICTURE OF MY PARENTS WITH THEIR
FIRST TELEVISION

I see them before the television, the proud owners
of a wooden case in which the four-o-five
presents its milky versions of success
with the last official faces of a time
that was always more dead than alive,
when Hanratty cleaned the windows and a crime
was solved by men with briefcases and bowlers,
when gentlemen made jokes in evening dress.

They fought their way to this, to Lady Barnett,
to Bernard Braden and John Freeman, Kathie Kay
and Alan Breeze, to all those names of power
that solved nothing but could somehow fill
the hours before they slipped away
to private lives that grew more private still,
past old reliable faces by which they set
their clocks precisely to the latest hour.

Some blurred depth in their eyes won't come to rest:
perhaps they're trapped in what they bought,
in all their trappings, in the slim white frame
of the square photograph they sent back home
to show the television. Now they're caught
and solemn. Slowly they become
the stillness by which they are both possessed.
They're listening intently for a name

that once had power, on lips that formed the sound
in darkened flats, in beds in which they slept
and touched each other. Some act of violence
has pitched them here before the screen.
The actors know their speeches, are adept
at pulling faces, know when to go. They've been
elsewhere and are there still, on neutral ground,
of which this patch of grey is evidence.

Those mentioned in the poem appeared on our screens along with Richard Dimbleby, Gilbert Harding, Barbara Kelly, Gerald Nabarro, Helen Shapiro, Billy Wright, the Beverley Sisters, the Kaye Sisters, Alma Cogan, Russ Conway, and the whole cast of the Billy Cotton Band Show. James Hanratty, the executed alleged A6 killer, was a window cleaner from our own district close to my piano teacher. "Murder Bag" with Raymond Francis as Inspector Lockhart provided the briefcases and respectable hats. "Sunday Night at the London Palladium" provided the smartly dressed gentlemen comics and the high-kicking Tiller Girls. My parents sat down together, without a qualm of conscience, to watch both "Miss World" and "The Black and White Minstrel Show" (they even went to see the live show and took us with them). They regarded the rise of Tommy Steele and Cliff Richard with a certain horror that later turned to affection. The boy has come a long way, they said on seeing Tommy Steele at the Palladium.

Then, as far as my father and I were concerned, there was sport. Television carried the cup final. I fell in love with the post-Munich Manchester United team while my father slowly came round to Tottenham Hotspur, which might have been down to the team's traditionally Jewish support (he had supported the "Jewish" team, M.T.K., in Budapest).

We were Englishing ourselves as best we could. Not that my mother ever did, not properly. It wasn't that she resisted, although she did sometimes: she simply found it impossible. It was like the food. Food is the last great tie to our origins. Hungarian food is rich with sour cream, spicy, full-bodied, all beef and pork and chicken, paprika and red cabbage, high heat and sharp acridity followed by overwhelming Viennese sweetness, intense with colour. The drink, too, is intense, dry *pálinka*, heavy red wine, fat sluggish beer. English food seemed to have no taste at all, no punch, no gravity, no sentiment, no hurt, either genteel and polite or brutally stodgy, nothing more than a matter of weight, either cucumber sandwich or toad-in-the-hole.

This was supposed to be the first station on the route to happiness, her own desired happiness, but it was also a journey away from herself. It was easier for us children. We followed Popeye and Bluto and Olive Oyl, we followed Disney, we followed the Lone Ranger and, when permitted to stay up, we followed "Wagon Train" down the Western trail at least until 9 p.m., when we were sent to bed. We, the children, were pioneers: they, the adults, were castaways, each in their own way, but my mother always the more conspicuous and, I suspect, the more lost.

28

Despite the complex, sometimes dizzy process of acclimatisation, my parents kept in touch with other Hungarians. There were a good many of them within bus or tube calling distance. There was the bohemian artist with his motorbike and hope of making a living through art, and his wife, the lovely, effervescent woman I fell in puppy-love with, and whom he was later to divorce. There was the lawyer in an office job and his wife who was currently working in a leather factory. There was the warm-hearted working-class couple who were to remain friends for life; there was the photographer and his family, there were the Fs, the Ts, the Ks and the Ms (he having been my father's fellow scout in Hungary). And there was the wealthy English couple they had first met in a Westgate street when the husband recognised my father from a *Thanet Gazette* photograph. They too were to remain lifelong friends.

My mother set out to befriend everyone. Despite her early difficulties with the language she wanted to do everything without my father's help. One day she looked to buy lungs at the butcher's, who asked her the name of our dog. Lights were for animals only in England but were a proper dish in Hungary. She told him we had no dog.

We were soon about to get one, a small yappy mutt that we called Puszi (or "kiss", in Hungarian) but which sounded exactly like "pussy" in English. Funny, said the little Chinese boy who heard us calling it. It looks like a dog but it's a pussy. No, it wasn't. My mother didn't like cats. Sly, selfish creatures without affection or loyalty, she said. Back in Budapest she had had a small white dog she loved, a sheepdog called a *puli* that had to go when I was born because it grew fiercely jealous. Puszi was an impulse birthday present for my brother. She did not consult my father;

she just bought it. The dog ravaged the neighbour's garden then ran off somewhere. There was nobody at home during the day. It must have got bored, or desperate.

The garden-ravaging dog was one minor problem, but there were other misunderstandings. Our next-door neighbours must have complained about something, possibly a rude word we had picked up somewhere. My mother was furious and told us to sing aloud in the garden using all the rude words we had at our command. She cared nothing about polite language and was not to be put in her place.

The pleasures extended. We bought bicycles and my brother learned to ride one in the street, my mother and father taking turns to push him until one day he ran into a lamp-post and broke his nose. We played outside with the neighbours' children, with Shirley and Helen and Jimmy and the older Frank who, a couple of years later, was to press a small book of nudie photographs into my hand. I hid them behind the piano. My mother discovered them and laughed.

On Sundays we went for lunch either at the local Italian café or, when we felt flush, to Schmidt's in Charlotte Street for a *Wiener schnitzel*. My brother began to learn the violin and took lessons from Mr S., a member of Mantovani's orchestra, who lived further up the hill in one of Ernest Trobridge's romantic castellated houses. My brother was talented. A visitor who turned up during one of his lessons couldn't tell who was playing, my brother or Mr S. I was doing well at primary school. Good marks!

Her firm ideas about dress could be hard on us. She abhorred the way the English dressed their children: the long flannel shorts, the sloppy woollen socks, the scuffed shoes, the thatch of hair, the greyness of it all. We had to wear white sandals and white socks. Your shorts will be short, continental length, she decided.

You will be dressed alike. Your hair will be neatly combed, she resolved. We were a laughing stock, but not to her. In any case, unlike my brother, I was beginning to develop rebellious habits. I started playing football in the playground and ruined the shoes so had to be given heavier duty brown shoes instead. My hair would not be combed right. I made friends with boys who took me bus-spotting but stole my father's stamps. Against all the odds I went with the school's Christian group to the Isle of Wight and returned a praying Christian. Religion didn't matter; clothes and school marks did. Becoming a Christian was rather good in its way. Why not forget the horrendous past, blend in and succeed? Become a Christian if you want. Believe in any old rubbish if it helps. But watch your clothes and school marks.

Because she was working, we could afford to pay a Yorkshire woman called Mrs Ivy to meet us from school, to give us a bite to eat and to stay with us until one or other parent got home, which could be as late as seven o'clock. Mrs Ivy was to allow us to watch a little T.V., but then we had to get on with our homework.

Mrs Ivy can't have been much older than my parents but already had grey hair and seemed an old woman to us. She was from Hull. Hull was another world.

At one point that same year, T., one of the Hungarian friends, made my father a business proposition. T. was a skilful mechanic. He had made contact with a Hungarian in Canada who told him all about automatic carwashes. There were no automatic carwashes in England. Why not invest in it? My father, with his famous managerial talent, could run the business side of things and T. could deal with the technical. My mother was firmly opposed to it as she was to most risks of that kind, at least if he was taking them. They could have been rich, according to my father As it happens T. got divorced and went to Canada.

There was no time to regret it. In the second year there we bought a car, a second-hand maroon Hillman Minx, chiefly to cope with the hill, but also out of sheer fascination. It was one T. had mended. It had sat in a garage for two years. It was perfect – cheap, with leather inside, and it lasted. If arrival in England was year zero we were doing pretty well by zero plus three.

29

It is good to think there were three years of exhilaration before the illness set in. Everything was new. Everything was bigger and better, at least in prospect. We would have had neither T.V. nor car in Hungary. Job security would have depended on unpredictable political currents. Now, for the first time, we had all we could want materially, both parents had steady jobs and we even managed a holiday in Hastings. We could go to the sea, as we never could in Hungary, and be reassured by the vastness all around us. The sea guaranteed there would be no shifting of borders. No foreign army would march in and overrun what Hungarians called "the island nation". The British Navy was the finest navy. The British Empire was the greatest the world had ever seen. Britain had won the war and here we were on the very beach where Britain had last been invaded. And when was that? Almost nine hundred years ago. Think of that! What was it that mattered most in England? Freedom, said my father. Freedom.

Everything was starting from scratch. Landing at Heathrow on board a B.O.A.C. Britannia refugee flight on the cold night of December 10, 1956, was point zero. We had zero. All we had were the clothes we had been wearing when we left, together with some others we had been given during our few days in Austria, plus our one luxury, the small hard case full of random photographs my mother had swept up from a chestful of such when we left so secretly and in such a hurry. The case had contained a toy typewriter, one of the childhood possessions I had to leave behind, and I had the task of carrying it across the border.

My father wore two coats but had a bad headache for which he was offered a cup of tea. Madam, I have a headache, he said to the kindly Red Cross woman. I don't need tea. I need aspirin. My father's reasonable competence in English was already making life easier. Three coaches were waiting to take some 120 of us to Tidworth army camp in Wiltshire, the barracks being free because the regiment was still in Suez. The army camp was our hotel, the barracks our dormitory for the next short period.

One day we were called into the barracks square where various clergy were waiting and asked us which of the religious groups we belonged to. This was clearly a matter of welfare rather than of worship. My mother was reluctant to join the Jewish party – some

50 out of the 120 turned out to be Jewish – but my father assured her there was nothing to fear in England and this time she accepted it. So the Jewish refugees were put on two buses and driven to the seaside, my father acting as interpreter on one of them.

It was dusk when the buses arrived in Westgate on the Kent coast, shortly before Christmas. The photographer from the *Thanet Gazette* was waiting for us. Since my father was the chief English speaker he was ushered to the front to meet welcoming dignitaries. The photograph appeared in the paper on December 21. My father is recognisable on the right but is not named in the caption. The woman sitting on the left might be my mother with my brother. Next to her, with his back to us, is a boy in a cap. That might have been me, but nothing is crystal clear save another woman with a baby in the background and the suit of the official. And my father, in profile, in a heavy winter coat.

The Jewish Refugee Council distributed pocket money and the families dispersed to their various bed and breakfasts. We went to the hospitable Mr and Mrs Pulford's establishment and remained there until the early spring, when another photograph was taken of the refugees with the Pulfords and their dog. The bohemian artist and his wife are in the picture I assume my mother must have taken. People are quite smartly dressed. The men have picked up suits and ties, the women are in simple but neat dresses.

My father continued to act as the principal interpreter while the debriefing and processing went on. My mother walked us along the sea front. None of us had seen the sea before. We attended language classes. We were taken to a great Christmas party at the Dorchester in London. We went on a visit to the circus. Winter was turning into spring.

We, that is my father and I, even went to the wrestling at Ramsgate; he was interpreting for one of the refugees who had

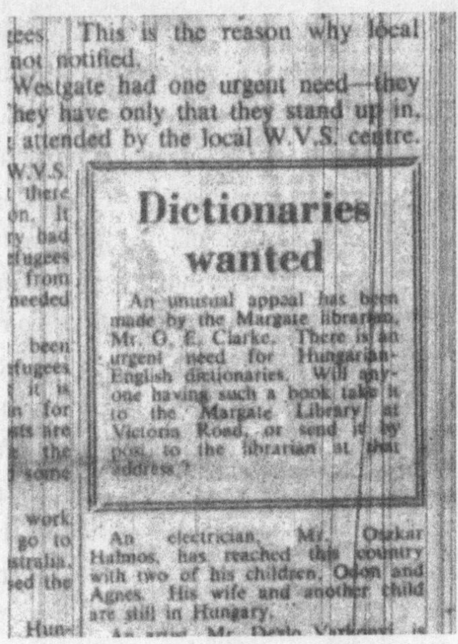

This is the reason why local not notified.

Westgate had one urgent need—they have only that they stand up in, attended by the local W.V.S. centre.

Dictionaries wanted

An unusual appeal has been made by the Margate librarian, Mr. O. E. Clarke. There is an urgent need for Hungarian-English dictionaries. Will anyone having such a book take it to the Margate Library at Victoria Road, or send it by post, to the librarian at that address?

An electrician, Mr. Oszkar Halmos, has reached this country with two of his children, Odon and Agnes. His wife and another child are still in Hungary.

chosen a career in wrestling. My mother refused the invitation. She had a younger child to look after and she hadn't come all this way to see violence, or indeed any sport at all. Sport was for grown-up children. Footballers were men acting like boys. The scrum in rugby, when she eventually got to see it on television, was a comical spectacle she called *segbebujósdi*. Adults hiding up each other's arses. Cricket was an English eccentricity, tedium, hardly sport at all, more like a kind of Morris Dancing. Life was a serious business in which childish amusements might have been appropriate for children but not for adults. She could joke about life, she could dance and appreciate art and she played board games with us with a fervency bordering on religious enthusiasm, but that was about family and childhood, neither of which were to be taken for granted. Not for one second.

Life was about survival first and foremost, but survival did not mean bending to the prevailing wind, which in any case was likely to be fierce. It was about standing up to it or banishing it. This was serious; it was for ever. Nevertheless there may be others out there whom one might love and even trust. She had no hesitation getting into conversations with people she had never met. She came on like a small one-woman army. She used her hands and eyes to communicate until the words and phrases began to fall into place, but even before then there was a place to be staked and a face to present.

Telling the story backwards, I am conscious of seeing and showing her as she was at the end of a process of which the beginning must remain a mystery to me. I can trace elements of madness and a furious desire for control which sounds oppressive, and indeed it was in some respects, but it was as impulsively generous as it was jealous. She would have given those she loved anything at all. She took to people as abruptly as she froze them out. I have no wish to submit her to retrospective analysis. I want to report her presence and register it as it moved through life by moving back into her own past with her. I want to puzzle over it and admire it while being aghast at it. I don't want to be certain of anything. I don't want to come to conclusions.

But I can't help thinking her generosity flowed both outwards and inwards, that she wanted to present herself to herself as generous, because that understanding was vital to her, because impulsive generosity had to exist in the world even if its immediate effects were sometimes oppressive. When we played Monopoly on those religiously kept family Sundays and our play money was running short, she was determined to lend us play cash. Go on, take it, she would insist and we would reject, and reject with an annoyance that could verge on guilty petulance. That's not the game, mum, we'd say, meaning: We don't want your pity because we don't want to play at being pitiable creatures in case we become pitiable creatures. Did she not feel the complexity when I was sixteen and she offered me her arm in the street, saying: Since you haven't got a girlfriend, I'll take your arm, and I yanked my arm away? Surely she must have sensed the conflict! I knew I was hurting her by rejecting her. Generosity and pity are closely linked in the mind of the receiver. Rejecting the "favour" and hurting the one who offers favour is itself hateful. We are hurt by our own hurting, but at least it is we ourselves who are the active agents in that. Always bite the hand that feeds you, says pride. That way it can't squeeze you.

Those early days in England must have been heady for her. At last she was far from danger, further from the memory of loss and inhumanity. She did not particularly like England, but she thought she was going to Australia and England was a vital staging post on the journey.

30

The great virtue of Australia was that it was not Europe, indeed that it was as far from Europe as one could possibly get. There, winter was summer and summer was winter. Improbable, delicate-looking creatures leapt through the air as if they had just arrived from another world. The world of Kanga and Roo, however childish (we had read *Winnie the Pooh* in Frigyes Karinthy's translation while still in Hungary), suggested a maternal role that would have appealed to her. Your children are in your pocket! You wash them, you tend them, then you leap into the great clear, hot air together as if freedom were your right and extended into infinity.

I am imagining this. The chief attraction would not have been the presence of kangaroos but the absence of monsters she knew all too well. The family in Australia was my father's, his cousin Annie, her architect husband Ervin, their children and their young family, all clearly prospering under the Sydney sun. She had reasons for being wary of my father's people, but a new world must mean a fresh start. Besides it was the one concrete practical solution. It had been the plan all along. The family was willing to offer us accommodation as well as the guarantee of a start-up job and that was all that was needed for a family to qualify for the £10 assisted passage. One just had to apply.

So we applied as soon as we could. My father registered his desire to go to Australia on the very night we arrived in England and then followed the necessary procedure. It was just a matter of waiting.

Among my father's papers after his death I discovered a sequence of letters that traced the process of application. The first is from Australia House on March 13, 1957. It informs my parents of the necessity of medical and X-ray examinations and covers the expense, at least until permission has been received. The two that follow bear the same date, May 13. Both are from the Jews' Temporary Shelter office in Aldgate. The first tells us that we have a berth on the S.S. *Sydney*, sailing on the 27th, and advises us to apply for a visa. The second cancels the berth saying Australia House cannot provide a visa in time, but assures us that as soon as the visa is issued "transportation to Australia will be arranged".

By July 30 the medical must have taken place because the letter from Australia House informs us that my mother's application has been rejected. No reason is given. But the case has been referred to Departmental Headquarters in Canberra for a decision. So we are offered hope, then suspense, then disappointment, then again a little hope. On September 25 we receive a letter from Canberra on blue airmail paper. Apparently there had been an objection to the permit on the 10th but now the objection has been withdrawn and we can go ahead. We prepare to leave. Then another wait, until November 18, when Australia House write again. "I would advise you that it is not the practice for the Office to inform unsuccessful applicants of the reasons why their applications have not been approved."

It's a cruel business. The tortuous correspondence, the encouragements then the refusals, the sheer length of the process, are witnesses to my parents' desperation. And it is her fault, she thinks. It is the state of her heart that prevents us. She wanted out of Hungary, but now we are stuck in England.

The house we are stuck in is the first proper house, the one in Kingsbury. We had been there since the second week of February. The W.V.S. Civil Defence office tells us: "We have been able to obtain some beds, bedding, floor covering, chairs and cupboards for your new house – also some china and saucepans."

So it could be worse. It was after the failure of Australia that she began to talk of suicide and exhorted us to go without her.

31

What did it feel like for them, for her, to land in a wholly unfamiliar country – an island furthermore! – that was never intended to be the destination. What did they imagine of Australia? What did she imagine of England? Regarding the English her advice to us was based on certain preconceptions. England was damp and inevitably foggy. The English were taller than us. They wore bowler hats. They were not snappy dressers unless they were upper class and the upper class was not the same as the traditional Hungarian gentry. They were laconic, undemonstrative, but fastidiously polite. In England it is the custom for gentlemen to open doors for ladies, so when we eventually went to school she instructed us to open the door for lady teachers, which I did, to the horrified amusement of my classmates until I stopped, to the disappointment of my lady teachers. It may not have been disappointment, of course, simply a higher, more mysterious version of amusement.

Where did my mother get her ideas about Englishness? Would it have been from films? From Jules Verne (I know she read Verne, as did my father)? It would certainly not have been from the Hungarian press whose news both in the few papers and on the radio was restricted to whatever the party thought appropriate. Nothing from there then. England would have been the Second World War and Churchill and the bombs that fell on Budapest, bombs that were welcomed by people like her. The bombs were British and American and it is unlikely she would have distinguished much between the two nations. Because she was still in Budapest on July 2, 1944, when the bombing began. Her deportation was not till the late autumn of that year.

Then, twelve years later, for the first time in her life, she gets on an aeroplane in a country neighbouring her own. The plane ploughs on in the darkness for two or three hours. By the time it lands in the wholly unknown place the future has become both concrete and provisional. This is not a country: it is a transit camp. The airport is cold and full of strange voices. There is the waiting for the bus that moves through further darkness, down country roads, towards a place that no-one has ever heard of, an army camp, to its big dormitory, to crisp but icy sheets and rough grey blankets. To rows and rows of beds. The temperature is below zero and it will get colder, down to –9C by February, but surely we will be elsewhere by then. This is December 10 moving on towards the 11th.

At least we are far from what she most fears and resists. We must play it by ear, but my father's knowledge of English must stand us in good stead. He is useful in these situations. He has held a position of some authority and can deal with officials. She has confidence in him in this respect. In any case, there is nothing she can do because she doesn't understand what is going on and he has to try and explain as best he can. He must speak for the four of us and is capable of doing so. She distrusts and resists authority, however, very much including his. It has its uses in the appropriate circumstances. The whole journey here has been dreamlike. But authorities, with their questions and answers, are awkward dream figures. One must keep one's wits about one in dreams, they so quickly turn into nightmares.

Then there is the sea as a thought that carries meaning even if you have never seen it. Hungarian fairy tales begin not with "Once upon a time" but with *Egyszer volt, hol nem volt, túl az Óperencián*, translated roughly as "Once there was, then there wasn't, somewhere beyond the great ocean . . ." The ocean is a myth the size of a real ocean. Any island is a fantastical place in the imagination, and Britain, being so much smaller than Australia, which was merely a continent albeit with fantastical creatures (and we were born and had spent our lives on a continent), was just such a fantastical place. Being an island was both a desirable and a feared condition. The Hungarian joke about islands asks whether it is good to live on an island. It turns out it is bad in that you have no neighbours, but then it is good too, for precisely the same reason. Hungary's neighbours were forever shrinking and expanding in Alice in Wonderland fashion. Maps show the border now here, now there, especially where my mother's birthplace was concerned. But here we were in Alice in Wonderland's own right-little, tight-little, topsy-turvy island, and out there, as we were to observe a few days later, lay the sea itself, dark, overwhelming, exotic and cold. When I asked my father for his first impression of the sea he was lost for words. Fantastic, he said and paused, then repeated, fantastic!

So this was where we were, this is where her instincts had landed us for now, this official, bus-load, barracks-load transit camp that we would soon get to meet along with all its pretty little terraced houses with their quizzical but perfectly friendly inhabitants. Friendly in their own inscrutable way, which was not her way, because, for her, her way was a form of truth, a necessity that had to speak up for itself, at least once it had begun to understand the language and this whole sea-sodden, salt-tasting place.

32

Another item amongst my father's papers is a signed form from the chief engineer of the Hungarian Ministry of Construction, dated December 1, 1956, certifying that my father has been sent to the engineering works at Győr, near the Austrian border, to take stock of the situation there regarding tools and materials, and to direct any spare workers to Budapest for important work in the capital.

This was certainly a pretext my father had invented and, as he tells it, his boss was playing along. In any case we were ready, packed for the border crossing, complete with a story we were to tell should anyone ask, the story being that while he was on a job he was taking this opportunity to bring his wife and sick children along for a few days' holiday.

The country was still in chaos. Budapest had been the scene of heavy street fighting and tanks had destroyed several buildings. Those who had fought in the revolution were in hiding or being rounded up. Many were to be executed. On the other hand, since most of the army, the police and the border force had gone over to the revolution, border security was still patchy and continued to be so until the end of the winter. More than 220,000 people were to find their way out of the country, and they were not just revolutionaries in fear of immediate arrest. We were among them.

There had in fact been fighting in our street. My brother and I were at home recovering from scarlet fever at the time and my mother was with us. The revolution had broken out on October 23, a Tuesday. My father was on his way home from work at the time. The A.V.H., the notorious state security police, were out in force. He had been delayed and, knowing my mother would be worried, he began to hurry. Once he got home they listened to the radio and heard there were demonstrations. Friends rang to ask him if he knew what was going on. One asked if there would be street fighting. My father said he didn't think so but advised him to stay indoors. There were families to look after. That evening, in his radio broadcast, the deputy prime minister referred to the demonstrators as a fascist mob. That seemed very unlikely. Later there were bulletins that said people with weapons had entered the radio building.

We ourselves heard gunfire the next day. By that time there had been deaths and martial law was declared. People with rifles and pistols were roaming the streets. There were rumours that leading communists were being rounded up. My father persuaded the janitor, who had locked the building, to let him out and he ventured up to the nearby main road, the Lenin Ring. My mother was shouting to him from the window to come back. He came home safely, then wanted to get out again the next day to check on his mother, his sister and aunts. My mother was bitterly opposed to it, but then one of the elderly aunts turned up at the door of the block. She seemed oblivious to the danger and had brought us some food. The shops were closed.

By Thursday the gunfire was closer, just down our street. One bullet flew in through the window, ricocheted off the ceiling and hit the toy watch I was wearing on my wrist. Further fighting was soon to follow, including the massacre in the square before Parliament. Someone in the block – a young man – was reported to have died. There were calls for revenge, crowds crying: "Get them! Hang them from the lamp-posts!" There were also rumours of anti-Semitic factions demanding Jewish blood. I imagine this did it for my mother. She feared particularly for my father who was generally known to be a Jew, while she was not. She suggested he escape on his own, that he should just pack a suitcase and go.

My father did not want to go. He felt he might be safe. But having heard that his personal files showed my mother's background and character and that that would limit his progress he realised his career had peaked. He also knew, as one of four prominent Jews in the ministry, that there had been calls for him to be sacked. In any case his job entailed wage control, bonuses and Stakhanovite work competitions. It was not a popular job. "No more Auschwitzes, let's finish the job here," went one rumoured mob chant. And indeed the leadership of the pre-revolution party, including the dictator Rákosi, his deputy, the minister of culture and the head of the A.V.H. himself, were all known to be undeclared Jews, old Moscow Jews or radicalised post-war Jews. They had changed their names, just as my father had changed his. All Communists were Jews, went one line of thought.

By this time Russian tanks were on the streets. We needed more food and a friend of my mother's, Irén, rang to say we should come over to her place in a more secure quarter. Seeing there were children involved, the soldiers might let us through. We could not get out of the block that day but it became possible the next. There were bodies in the street and people hanging from lamp-posts. I suffered nightmares for weeks after, according to my father. We walked under the barrel of a Russian tank, but the Russians did not stop us. Irén welcomed us with food and her two Great Danes. Her architect husband had left her for another woman and was not there.

We stayed in her cramped flat for two or three days, then, it being quieter on the 28th, a Sunday, we went home. It was that evening the revolutionary prime minister, Imre Nagy, announced the withdrawal of Russian troops as well as the disbanding of the dreaded security police. Those troops, or rather a different regiment, returned at dawn on November 4 after everyone thought the revolution had won, and, after bloody battles and street fighting, it was the end of serious resistance.

My father thought the fascist mob would be crushed for good now, but my mother did not agree. If the borders were open we should go, and go quickly. The only problem was the children, still in quarantine with scarlet fever. That had to be discussed with the neighbourhood doctor, who insisted on a delay.

One night my parents and some friends were discussing their plans for leaving and had left a big map of Hungary and the countries that bordered it open on the floor. I had woken up and was playing with the map, stepping from one country to the next. One had only to walk, after all. We were well enough now.

33

It was as well we had a story for the train because soldiers were moving up and down it and we had suitcases and looked conspicuously well dressed, my brother and I in long velvet trousers and velvet tops! We spent the night in a hotel and my father went to the works he was supervising. The man there asked him straight out if we were wanting to leave. He promised to say nothing about it and advised us not to get the train all the way to the border city of Sopron, but to get off a stop or two before, possibly at Fertőboz where, so he had heard, villagers were guiding people across the border. This was another tense journey. A distant relative of my father was on the same train and asked to sit with us as part of the family should we be questioned. At some point she left and we did not see her again. Fifteen or so other people got off at the same stop as we did, at about five in the afternoon. It was a tiny village. An old man came up to us straight away and asked us if we wanted to go to Austria and, if so, would we like him to take us there. He and his friend would take us across. He named no price and simply asked for whatever we could give. He made the same offer to the others.

He led everyone to a barn in his yard and told us to wait there. One person was delegated to collect whatever we had and we were told to keep silent because the border guards maintained a half-hourly patrol. We were about six kilometres from the border, he said. We were to light no matches and children had to be kept quiet. My brother was only three and a little fretful, but my parents had some sleeping potion left over from the scarlet fever, so they gave that to him.

The old man returned at around midnight. None of the adults had slept. He told us that he and his friend would lead the group and a third would bring up the rear in case anyone got lost. It would be slow progress, he said. My father remembered it as a terrible journey in freezing cold, over mud and through a wood. My mother could no longer carry her suitcase of clothes, so my father told her to drop it. He carried my brother on his back, I laboured along with my small bag, falling into a ditch at one point, as did my mother. At least there was no snow. Then my father dropped his suitcase and it burst open. He had time to recover only half his things before moving on.

The journey took two or three hours. Then the old man pointed to some lights ahead and told us that was the Austrian border post. My father gave him his watch and any remaining Hungarian money we had, then the old man and his two friends disappeared into the trees. There was an embankment to climb to the paved road. The others had gone on and we were the last. My mother had to be pulled up the embankment. She was exhausted. My father's suitcase was also gone by now. The road was surrounded by ditches. The first thing my father did on reaching the road was to throw his party card away. An Austrian border guard appeared and my mother burst into tears.

It was another half an hour's walk and early morning by the time we arrived at the camp on the main Wiener Neustadt road. Everyone was pretty numb by then. A nurse escorted us to a prefab building containing iron beds and mattresses. We were advised to lie down and get some sleep, they would talk to us in the morning.

In the morning we were shown to a reception room where we were met by two women, one very young and beautiful and particularly concerned for my brother and me. She was a princess or countess, said my father, possibly called Fürstenberg. If that was the case she would have been the sixteen-year-old Ira von Fürstenberg, later an Italian film star, who had Hungarian connections. She immediately saw to it that we got some blankets and clothing. After the overnight walk through the mud it was chiefly shoes we needed. My father told her we wanted to go to Australia. She said that was unlikely because Australia had set a quota and, it being early December, the chances were the quota would be full. My father explained about his cousin, so she suggested he go to Vienna and talk to the Australian Embassy. She immediately lent him the train fare and gave him a lift to the station.

There was, my father said, a huge queue at the embassy, but he waited and eventually got to speak to someone who was firmly of the view that we could not go to Australia. The quota was full and even people with permits were being turned down.

At the camp the next morning the princess suggested we go to England. Australia being a member of the Commonwealth, it might be easier from there. There were a number of caravans in the camp with various international flags on them. My father went to the British caravan and joined the queue. Once inside he saw a British army officer and a woman interpreter, and he heard the officer tell the interpreter: Ask him to sit down. He sat down before she could translate and explained that he understood every word, and though his English was only sufficient for basic things, the interview could be conducted without the need for translation.

The officer was surprised, said my father, but then listened while he explained our situation. When he heard my father was in plumbing, heating and ventilation and had worked in the ministry, he was clearly pleased and declared my father would have no problem finding work in Britain, and if he didn't like it, we could proceed to Australia. There it was. It was like magic.

My mother was delighted. The next morning, before breakfast, another young woman burst in and told us to be ready in ten minutes for the coach to the airport. We didn't have much to pack but were still the last aboard. In the hurry I left one of my shoes behind and so arrived in England with only one shoe. But I was clad in velvet.

34

Goodbye Hungary, goodbye Central Europe, goodbye history. The last few weeks had rushed past. Between the idea of leaving and the actual departure there would have been no more than three weeks. A whole revolution had begun and ended in that time. But this was life as one had learned it. Life, as learned, was composed of relatively brief episodes, each seeming an eternity at the time, none of them suggesting stability, let alone permanence. Short span, short breath.

How to divide up the time between my birth and our departure?

Let me move backwards a little at a time.

Sometimes she was home in the flat, on the third floor of an inner-city block facing the Liszt Music Academy. We had been very lucky to get it because space in the capital was limited and much was still in ruins after the war. Communism had brought agricultural workers in from the country and was turning them into industrial workers. They had to live in barracks and sleep on bunks or find whatever accommodation they could get. This flat had three rooms: a bedroom for my parents, a room for my brother and me, and a large sitting room in between complete with dining table, a vitrine, an intarsia table and, miraculously, a baby grand piano, all these being recovered items previously stolen from the flat of Uncle Sándor, the stockbroker, one of father's richer murdered uncles.

The windows looked out into a street which was neither too narrow nor too wide. I cannot remember a lift, at least not a lift that was working, but the stairs were not too steep and my mother could rest between floors. The walls of the stairwell were covered in children's chalk drawings. The courtyard was in the janitor's care and had nothing special in it like a well or a garden or a statue as some courtyards did, but once the block gates were shut it was quiet with its own square of sky. There were two floors above us, but I don't remember ever venturing up there.

All kinds of people lived in the block, from professionals and academics to workers, from bus drivers through to navvies. Each block was a cross-section of Budapest society. There were no rich – if there were any they would have been the party elite and would have lived in villas in the steep leafy streets of Buda on the other side of the Danube. This was Pest: busy, urban, commercial, industrial, bureaucratic, factory-and-office-patched, cinema-and-store-and-café-riddled Pest.

Franz Liszt tér just round the corner, now a buzzing square with cafés and restaurants, with ornamental paving and lined with trees, was bare in the Fifties, with only a small children's sandpit. I remember because that was one of the places in which I played and because my mother took a number of large portrait photographs of me there. They all show me at the height of sartorial elegance.

The Art Nouveau façade of the Music Academy was imposing, even a trifle threatening with the great enthroned figure of Franz Liszt glaring down. My primary school was a few blocks in the other direction. It's still there near the old Writers Club called the Fészek, or Nest. I could walk down to the school by myself and come back in the early afternoon. Most days my mother would not be there but at *Esti Budapest*, the daily evening paper, the last place she worked in Hungary. An older woman up from the country, who had once done similar work for the murdered relative, would be waiting for me. Éva was employed to clean and cook, not to teach us to swear, nor did she go out of her way to teach us, she just swore naturally and we learned anyway. Later, when she grew weaker, she asked to return to her home village and a pretty young woman called Marika took her place. But this was very near the end of our time in Budapest.

35

My mother was a photographer. It was the single word used to describe her in 1945 when she was transferred from Ravensbrück to Penig. But we have to crawl back further for that. In 1956 *Esti Budapest* was a popular evening paper, and she was not so much a news photographer as a laboratory worker, only going out on group assignments. That would have been a disappointment to her, but there were likely reasons. The overt reason was her heart condition. She had fainted once or twice when out with her camera and was therefore thought to be a risk. But she was a risk in another way too.

After the takeover of the Moscow-backed Hungarian Workers Party in 1949 there was the usual reign of terror accompanied by the usual purges, the usual arrival of a car in front of the block and the fear of the knock on the door in the night. That year had seen the arrest of one of the leading figures in the party, László Rajk, on the charge of being a spy for Marshall Tito, the leader of the Yugoslav Communist Party that had just fallen out with Moscow. Rajk had fought in the International Brigade in Spain and was responsible for setting up the security police and for the suppression of various institutions and religions, as well as the arrest of anyone who fell under suspicion, but he was not a Moscow man. He was tortured, made to plead guilty, and hanged. This was part of a great wave of arrests and trials intended to demonstrate the "justified fear" of sabotage and possible insurrection. If there were no plots, you had to invent them.

Like everyone else at that time, right up to the revolution, my mother and father were expected to file confidential reports on their colleagues at work, knowing full well that their colleagues were doing the same for them. These would involve accounts of suspicious conversations or indeed any sign at all of discontent. My father's way was to agree and to file as bland a report as he could: his way was not my mother's way though. She was confrontational. She simply said no, she would not do it. She said it to a senior officer in the security police. She told him why, too – that she had not supported socialism in order to spy on her friends.

Nor was she prepared to act as a propagandist, which entailed calling on local people, distributing leaflets, explaining directives, telling them how splendidly everything was going and asking their opinions. She couldn't persuade herself that all was well when there were shortages, so she refused outright, saying she was too busy.

This could have led to serious trouble for her, but my father had been in the ministry since 1950. There were only three people above him in rank and he was clean. He was prepared to do some propaganda work. In the climate of the times people were scared to talk to him so he could honestly state that they never complained. Besides, he was from a working-class family and was doing everything right. She was from a middle-class family and had been refused party membership on those grounds when she applied. She was not a class enemy, simply a class alien. Maybe my father's status offered some protection. Neither of them were important people, but he, at least, was useful. While his position might have protected her, hers did him no favours.

My mother was nothing if not courageous and would not have allowed physical weakness to prevent her working as a photographer. That was what it said on the Penig list: not lab technician, photographer. The few times she spent at home working at her light-box would have been deeply frustrating for her. No wonder she hit me once with one of my school books when my homework wasn't quite neat enough. I hadn't applied myself properly. She was crouched over the light-box. She should have been out doing what she wanted to be doing and had trained for.

My father had certainly worked hard. The party had decided he should study for a degree in Economics so he was attending classes three nights a week at the Karl Marx University. But everyone was working as hard as they could. It was the time of production norms and those norms would be raised through the efforts of the most productive. My father knew about that since he was in charge of administering part of it.

Nevertheless, he was proud of his position. It was against all expectations for the son of a shop-floor worker in a shoe factory. The party had recognised him, which was more than my mother had. Her attitude to his career, as he admits, was determined by her basic attitude to all such things. She warned him not to get above himself. "Don't think, my dear, that you are so brilliant! Don't think you are fantastic! Things just happened to you! You're just a little man, like all the rest!" There was one time he was on the telephone to his mother and he seemed to be boasting to her that he had had to exert his authority and get someone sacked. His mother was, she thought, egging him on so she tore him to strips at the end of the conversation. My father wished in hindsight she had been a little more supportive. "One needs sometimes to be praised, to be told that one is good and successful. Not that I was great or powerful, but considering my circumstances I hadn't done badly."

36

"In the summer of 1949 there began the process of nationalisation of all companies that employed more than ten people. I was in my office with Béla and his sister-in-law Sári, who did the wages – it was summer, about 11 a.m. – when three people walked in. One was from the council and the other two were from the local party. They handed an ultimatum to Béla, as the owner of the company, giving him one week to close down operations. Then he would be notified what to do with the men and materials. He was not to take anything from the workshop, no materials, no money, no machinery, no furniture, nothing. From then on one of the three came in every morning to supervise the process and the making of an inventory.

"This went on for three or four days, then I was given a piece of paper which told me to report to the local party office. Of course I was concerned, not knowing what lay in store for me (my friend was, after all, the owner of the company), but I reported there in the morning and they explained to me that they regarded me as a working-class man, an experienced leader of a company, capable both mechanically and organisationally, and that this company would be amalgamated with four others to form a new nationalised company to be called the Általános Szerelő Vállalat, (the General Mechanical Services Company). The offices would be on fashionable Madách tér. They even told me that the chief engineer, and thereby deputy head of the company, would be one of the owners of the old companies, and that I would have to be vigilant in case he did anything against the interests of the party or the state, such as attempt to sabotage the works. I was to become their trustee. These party men were youngish, very drab, very solemn.

"Béla was shattered, Sári even more so. She was quite an outspoken woman, he tended to be more cautious. She was offered nothing and was simply kicked out. He, because of his obvious expertise, was offered a job at another nationalised company made up of five smaller private firms. They made sure he would not be at the same company as I was, nor with his old workforce.

"They closed down the workshop. The machinery and materials were brought into another yard and I was introduced to a by-then already functioning company whose director used to be a plumbing foreman. This man was a simple, kind plumber. The man I was to keep an eye on was a Jew, Rónay – and he was the deputy head. I was introduced to them in the presence of the local party secretary, who called me in and said, 'Comrade Szirtes (I was Szirtes by then and had been since summer '45) will be the leader of a new department to be known as the Üzemgazdasági Osztály (Manpower and Statistical Department), a kind of planning office.'

"So there I was. I had no idea what such work involved. I was given a young woman as a secretary and a young man to do all the paperwork. Somehow or other I succeeded in grasping what they wanted. It meant doing a lot of reports and statements which were to go to the ministry, who could keep tabs on progress and personnel. I was not the personnel department as such – they had one of those too, to check the reliability of the workers – I was essentially in charge of figures. Very quickly I was promoted to my position at the ministry. I had become somebody.

"I was the leader of a nation-wide department dealing with all the companies involved with plumbing, central heating, electrical installations, lifts and the hire of small items of building equipment. All these companies belonged to our section of the ministry, or *főosztály*. There were six sections within the main one and I was leader of one of them. My job entailed working out principles, carrying these principles down through committees who then transmitted them to the companies. These principles became codes of practice, the laws of the trade. I was also responsible for workers' education, for organising the *munkaverseny*, or labour competition, and for calculating rates of pay. All incomes, salaries and bonuses earned by the directors of the nationalised companies were sanctioned by the ministry. By me. So I knew what everyone at the top of a company was earning.

"Above me was the head of the state department in charge of all nationalised companies dealing with plumbing, central heating and electrical installation. It was a highly politicised post. Only those with a high political status or a top trade qualification were eligible for it. Above him came the deputy minister, then the minister himself.

"Practically all my colleagues had gone through the same kind of process. We were a new class of administrators. Very few were from the old generation who were only kept on because of their technical expertise.

"I was expected to participate fully in political matters. There was at least one weekly meeting, plus two meetings per month of the party-political wing of the ministry, and two per month of the trade union. Everyone had to belong to the union, and everyone had to go to all the meetings. Looking back on it, the meetings were not a complete waste of time.

"At party meetings the party secretary would usually be at the head of the table, and would give a talk about recent political events. Of course it was very biased, I can say that now, but when I was there and took part, I accepted it. He would talk for about half an hour, then there would be questions followed by the delegation of certain tasks.

"At union meetings the emphasis was on work and production. It began with the head of department's evaluation of the work in hand and the performances of sections and individuals within sections. Then we discussed the work before us.

"By attending such meetings we developed aims and learned how to criticise and face criticism. We had to get up and answer each criticism in public. In addition we had to practise as much self-criticism as possible. Everyone was there down to the typists and filing clerks and all took part. It was good for them to be aware of everything that was happening.

"These meetings took place throughout Hungary in every industry, in every office and factory.

"There was another kind of meeting too. Once a week, about half an hour before starting work, everyone had to gather in small units to discuss and evaluate the political events of the past week and what the papers had to say about them. We had to read articles, to criticise and to voice our own opinion about what was happening in the country and in the world at large. These were highly political meetings, headed by the various sections. In my section I was the leader. I had quite a lot of enthusiasm for this in the beginning – later they piled on more and more meetings and I got tired of it, but you couldn't say too much against it, because this was the party line and you had to toe it. By the mid-Fifties, once they had selected me to attend extra-mural evening courses at the university, I found it exhausting.

"I began to feel trapped. I wanted to be nearer to production. Whenever I visited a building site I was received as a member of the ministry: I was guided and flattered, but I never got near the work force. My strength was organisation and I didn't need to organise much where I was. I was in the ministry's good books through sheer hard work, not through party activism. My colleagues believed their own propaganda: they were utterly brainwashed. I don't think of myself as being amongst them. I had a certain pride in my job, of course, but this had begun to pall. I saw I couldn't go any further. I had no career opportunities."

My father's words from our taped conversations. His rise from plumber's mate and book-keeper to leader of a department in the ministry was extraordinary and must have been dizzying for him. No wonder my mother wanted to keep his feet firmly on the ground. No wonder she told him: You are nobody.

37

She was in and out of the flat. On New Year's Eve in 1955 my parents were invited to a feast at the ministry and decided to take us with them. It was an icy night and snow lay on the streets. There were great tables put out in the big hall, there was music and conversation between bright-red faces. A pig's head was brought in on a platter. It felt wonderful to be out so late.

On the way home she began to dance, executing a modest few steps on the snow. There was no-one else there: the city was absolutely silent. For a moment she became someone quite different, not my mother but a woman independent of me. The sense of her as a woman rather than my mother must have been a complicated thought for a child, perhaps it was no more than an intuition.

One day when my mother was at home, I don't remember exactly when, she told me she was going to surprise my father. She was going to pretend to be a man. She said she would be dressed as a man and wear a false moustache. I was not to betray her. She went out and my father returned from work. Soon after there was a ring at the door and there was my mother, a man. The "man" claimed to have a message for my father. My father greeted her politely and invited her to sit down. My mother sat opposite him talking in a deep voice, but I gave the game away by crawling onto her lap. A game is what it was. There would have been a reason or occasion for it.

One reason might have been the recent visit from local party representatives following Nikita Khrushchev's secret speech at the XX Party Congress, in which he criticised Stalin. News of it got out and the party had to prepare its faithful. My father was informed at work and the local party went from flat to flat that same day. She was at home and I was with her. It was news to her.

We had a popular photograph of the genially smiling Stalin on the wall. He was after all the hero who had saved us: the whole nation had stopped work and wept when he died in 1953. My mother rejected the new official line and held me up to the photograph declaring that Stalin was a great and good man, telling me I was to love him whatever people might say. You can't go from hero to villain from one moment to the next.

38

First she had me, then, on March 19, 1952, she had András, Andrew as he was to become in England. According to my father they were out dancing a few days before he was born. If that is true I can't imagine that would have been his idea. She was admitted to hospital and expected to stay longer than the standard seven or eight days. There was no question in those days of fathers attending a birth and he carried on working as usual. When my brother was just a few days old he returned home at lunchtime to find Nana Éva, our daily help, in a panic because I was in severe pain. It was my stomach. My father thought it was probably constipation. Apparently I had been trying to go to the toilet but couldn't. I was three and a half years old and pretty strong, he thought, so he sat down to lunch and prepared to visit my mother in hospital. But my pain grew worse and so he hurried up to the fourth floor to the doctor who lived there. I wasn't one to complain as a child. The doctor was having his lunch too and told my father to go home and that he would be down soon. So my father rang the hospital to say he would be a little late and waited. He waited an hour, but the doctor did not come. Eventually, a couple of hours later, he appeared. He took one look at me and called the ambulance which set off to the same hospital, to a ward one floor below my mother's.

I was diagnosed with a case of life-threatening peritonitis. My father rushed upstairs to her and told her about the pain I had suffered, but not about me being in hospital. He said I was fine. She was dubious. Are you telling me the truth? she said. Why do you ask? he said. Something in your voice, she said. Meanwhile a nurse appeared and my father took the opportunity to run back downstairs to find out what was happening to me. I needed an emergency operation, he was told. Stay with your wife, said the doctor, and come back after visiting hours. My father did so, and was with her until ten at night. He remained in hospital until twelve, went home to rest for a couple of hours, then returned.

My mother's night was disturbed. She spent the time walking up and down the hospital corridors then, early in the morning, rang home to ask about me. My father wasn't there, of course. He's on his way to see you, said Nana Éva. But it was only eight o'clock on a Sunday morning. In the meantime I needed blood and one of my father's aunts was sent for to give some. It was ten in the morning by that time, my mother was frantic with worry, and did not yet know I was in the hospital a floor below hers. About noon my father was assured that I was over the crisis and he told her what had happened. She immediately hurried down to see me.

I was to spend three or four weeks in hospital and she more or less moved in to spend the nights with me, bringing Andrew with her. She would not leave me.

39

When at last I was discharged from hospital she went back to work where there was a crèche for Andrew. I was recovering at home with Nana Éva. Nana Éva was a village girl who had come to Budapest to find work and did so with murdered Uncle Sándor. Now she was fifty, unmarried and without a job. She wanted to go home to the village but needed money, so my parents took her on and paid her what they could out of their combined wages until she had enough. She had a room of her own in a flat some five minutes' walk away, so did not need to live in. She cleaned and cooked and baby-sat. I tried to half remember, half imagine her in a poem in the collection *Reel*.

The daily swore like a trooper, but cleaned and cooked
While the parents worked elsewhere, back in the age
Of Uncle Joe Stalin. She was how things looked

In the early Fifties. She occupied centre-stage
With her loose tongue, and they acted horrified
When the children erupted in foul language.

It was comical. Grandmother would have died
To hear it, being a respectable working-class
Woman who ran to a little cleaning on the side,

And as for grandfather, he was dead, alas,
The socialist playwright of the shop-floor
Swept off to Auschwitz in a cloud of gas.

Small rough hands she had, and a pinafore.
Her nose was snub, her teeth yellow and black
With cigarettes. She would lie down and snore

On the sofa most afternoons, flat on her back,
Then give them a cuddle and some kind of sweet,
And all the rooms were clean as if by magic.

She taught them *fuck* and *fart*, their mouths replete
With her tongue and her bad teeth in their heads,
Then disappeared back down into the street,

Their bodies tucked like small flames in their beds.

Her mind had begun to go by 1956 so she went back to the village.

40

A photograph of me aged about two in a double-fronted waistcoat, with shirt and tie, with perfectly combed hair. My mother's writing on the back:

> *Te voltál a kis vigasztalom, ha bántottak, ha fájt valami csak te tudtál vigasztalni, csak tebenned találtam vigasztalmat, drága kis mókuskám*
> "You were my little consolation, when they hurt me, whenever I ached, it was you alone who could console me, in you alone did I find consolation, my darling little squirrel."

That is a lot of consolation for a lot of pain. There is no defence against it: there is only time.

41

The clothes she dressed us in! I don't know whether the party took a view on appropriate daily wear. I know my father wore a trilby while most manual workers wore berets, and that he always wore a suit even when not at work while they wore overalls and heavy boots. But as for us, the children, we were more than elegant: we were out of this world. I had a stripy tank top and a miniature trench coat with matching peaked cap. My shoes had an unearthly shine. I had a two-piece three-button suit (without lapels) complete with both belt and a tiny tie with a doggy motif. A neat white handkerchief, perfectly folded, protruded from my top pocket. There was another peaked cap to go with that. All very *gamin*, all very *parisien*. White sandals were *de rigueur*. My brother was the perfectly dressed baby and toddler. She took a photograph of him by a park bench with some kind of pole nearby. It won a photographic competition and became a china figurine, one or two of which might still be extant somewhere.

His pram was quilted, a proper baby carriage. Then there was the velvet. For both of us. One outfit consisted of a zip-up jacket and dungarees, with yet another peaked cap. A few years later I am in a city square in Tyrolean shorts and a short-sleeved white shirt buttoned to the neck. I look as wise as Solomon. I look like a consolation.

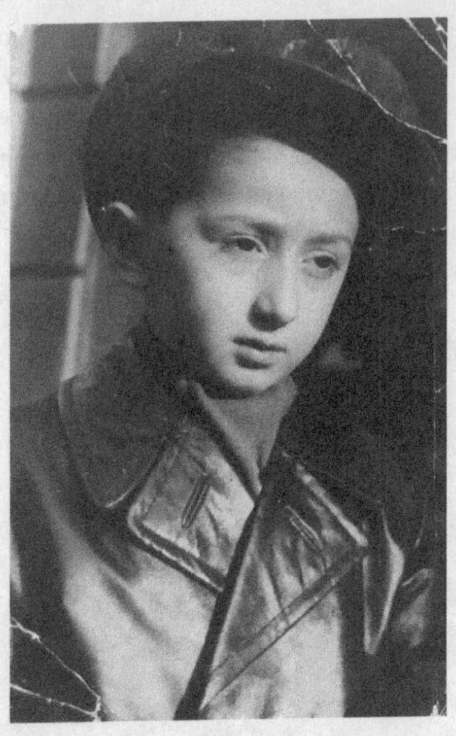

And see! There I am again in a full-length leather coat with a leather peaked cap, like a spy, decidedly like a spy. In another I am sitting with my first piano teacher, in a beautifully patterned waistcoat with a crisp white shirt and tie. It's the same waistcoat as I am wearing – my brother beside me in an identical waistcoat – at the refugee Christmas party at the Dorchester in London in 1956. And there are the velvet trousers in which I must have crossed the border.

How expensive was all this? How conspicuous? How aware was she of the sheer spectacle we provided? How much did she care?

She didn't care. She can't have done.

42

She herself is in the full flower of her beauty. She must have been startlingly attractive when she first arrived in Budapest, but now she is a young queen. She is still in her twenties. She is headstrong, playful, passionately loving and badly scarred. She shows her contempt for the world by swirling her gypsy skirt. She dismisses the demands of the paper. She dismisses the demands of the security police. She disdains the ministry. She tells death and misery to go hang themselves. But there remains the pain – the pain of contempt, rejection and devastating loss – for which she needs the intense consolation that only a child can provide.

When Andrew was born we were living in a flat above the puppet theatre. It was a four-room flat, of which we were entitled to use two. Shared flats were common, and in this case the original owner had vanished. In the room by the kitchen lived an old woman. There was a living room in the middle, with us on one side and a Jewish couple on the other, the man being a teacher. It was hardly convenient for them because, to get to their room, they either had to go through the bathroom or through the living room, which had officially been allocated to us as our second room, since I had been born by then and we were a family. My mother was very good in such situations. She accepted them and made an effort to be friends. There was in any case no way of arguing one's way out of it. It would have been regarded as a black mark for the complainant.

My mother's jobs are confusing. In the first years after the war she had a job at Operafotó, a photographic studio in town, and she would pick me up from the nursery on her way home. Later she found work at an architect's office. In between there was the newspaper job at *Esti Budapest*.

Her political status was confusing in other ways too. She was either not a member of the party because of her class background (middle-class Transylvanian, hence a class alien) or because her own behaviour prevented her becoming a full member. My father would have preferred her to be a member like him (reassuring working-class background) and accompany him to party meetings, to marches and to canvassing, something he did in the evenings and on Saturdays. He was already at the ministry and these would have been reassuring signs for the party.

Operafotó didn't last because ever fewer people had the money to spend on studio photography. There were only two of them there, she and her boss, and they could talk quite freely. But once she moved to the newspaper, a party organ like every other, she was aware of having to be more circumspect. She must have managed this some of the time, but she took the frustration of it out on my father. The picture team at *Esti Budapest* numbered just four, three men and her, and she worked as much in the lab as out on assignments.

What was my parents' social life like? It consisted chiefly of going to the cinema or meeting friends, though on rare occasions they could afford to go to the opera or, in my father's case, to a football match, though he did not like to leave her alone. She had one or two close female friends, including Irén and Rózsi, the wife of my father's last private employer, the plumber Béla. My father had some friends who had survived the work camps in which he served during the war as well as some from school or scout days. Beyond that there were cheap books and the short-range radio that could receive only Hungarian broadcasts limited to official news.

The move to the larger flat on the third floor, on the corner of the street opposite the Music Academy, was a great relief. It had three rooms and no fellow lodgers. My father had to do a lot of asking around at the ministry to find it. It took a few months but, though bare and ordinary enough in terms of size, it seemed like the height of luxury when we moved in.

That flat is the first home I remember. It was at the end of the courtyard corridor. There was a very small hall or vestibule that led to a bigger space, an inner hall without windows. The kitchen opened to the left, the bathroom was next to the kitchen and, beyond the kitchen, there was a small maid's room with its own window onto the courtyard. Nana Éva slept there occasionally once we moved. The furniture came from Uncle Sándor, though it had vanished from his own smart flat, as the furniture of the dead usually did, and so it had to be tracked down. People simply stole any furniture that was not quickly claimed. In this case one man had taken it all. My father found him, called on him, frightening him with two party officials. There it all was: the baby grand piano, the beautiful sideboard, the oval intarsia table, the vitrine and the dining table with its four chairs. Passing through the inner hall there was a big room with two windows where my parents slept at night on a sofa-bed but which, during the day, was the living room where the intarsia table, the vitrine and, above all, the piano found a place.

The piano was by far the most glamorous object. You could hide under it, embrace its carved legs, see your reflection in it, climb on it and, of course, play it. It was

> . . . a hybrid creature with only
> Three legs and a faint ephemeral grin,
>
> With feminine curves, a gorgeous womanly
> Voluptuousness . . .

The grinning keyboard grew to be a stern mistress too. My earliest memory of being naked as a child is inextricably linked to the form and gloss of the piano.

Leading off to the right through double doors was a smaller room where my brother and I slept and where we were to be confined during our initial attack of scarlet fever. Between the rooms my parents had slung a swing for us to play on.

> . . . The swing could be hooked up out of the way
> When not in use. Only an adult hand
>
> Could take it down and make the whole flat sway.
> Mother and father were gods of limited space.
> Only they could willingly fade away
>
> Like the child's own faintly breathed-on, mirrored face.

There was a large ceramic stove between the rooms as was common at the time. This too became an object of fantasy.

> . . . The stone sweats
> And sighs with the wind in the frozen northerly
>
> Forests we read about where dogs and cats
> Are children in disguise. Life goes up in flames,
> The familiar is swept under magic carpets.
>
> Their gingerbread-brown is focus for our games.
> We creep up on each other. We touch the tiles
> With drops of water that glitter like tiny gems
>
> Sizzling into silence . . .

She was queen of this domain and we were tenants of it. We even had that rare luxury, a telephone.

Here too she would have days when she worked at home. Although I was her one and only consolation, was clearly bright and a star pupil at primary school, there were times she lost her temper with me. I was a very early reader and writer but we had to master neat handwriting in exercise books covered in blue sugar paper, with a label stuck precisely in the middle but higher than the centre. The subject and our name we had to write there ourselves in our neatest hand. Inside the book itself (there were books with blank pages, books with lined pages and books with squared pages) the custom was to train our hands by getting us to draw decorative borders in folk motifs at the top and bottom of the page. There were hearts and tulips in colour – in red and blue and green. I must have messed up or showed some indifference because that was the occasion she rose from her light-box and hit me across the head with the schoolbook nearest to hand.

43

What happened then? Did she sit down again and continue her work? Did I cry or was I too shocked? Did she do as she often did with my father, offer tenderness and deep remorse after striking or shouting at him? What exactly had I done anyway to rouse her to such fury? I don't think I ever doubted that she loved me, not even at that moment. She would tell us, her children, often enough that she did so, so often in fact that I began to feel guilty for not loving her as much or as demonstratively, with so much clear devotion and with so many clear proofs. Did she in fact say (I believe she did) the fateful words: "You will never love me as much as I love you." And if she did (yes, she did) what was she hoping to achieve by it?

The articulate questions of the adult are not the questions of childhood but questions of some sort begin to form themselves even in a young child's mind. Reflecting on that "greater love" I think I feel very much now as I did then; that "you will never love me as much as I love you" was something she needed to say, not because she wanted to make us feel guilty but because she herself felt it to be so, and felt it with such urgency that she had to say it or die.

Beside the friends there was family. The favoured side, my father's two maiden aunts, were regular visitors. His sister had moved out to the provinces with her husband and their baby. His mother was *persona non grata*. His father had died in Auschwitz.

There remained the cousins the war and the camps had spared, but they were few. Her own family was dead, wiped off the face of the earth.

1949 was the great year of show trials and executions, the year the party took a firm grip on the country. It was a time of hardship and paranoia, of arrests at dawn, of vanishings and tortures, of what the newly installed dictator Mátyás Rákosi called "salami tactics", whereby they took rival parties and sliced them to pieces through the courts on various trumped-up charges that led to prison or work camp or death.

But this was not daily life for the average citizen. My father was "faintly aware" that such things happened, he told me, but he did not dwell on them because his own career was moving forward. He was a member of the newly amalgamated Social Democrat Party and the Communist Party under the new name of the Hungarian Workers' Party (essentially the communists under a new name). My mother was only a provisional member of the new governing party but she found work and they were able to start a family. They survived. Almost anything was better than what had gone before.

I cannot speak as a witness of my first two or three years. I can speak of sunlight in the flat, of sitting on the sofa and reading, of having boxes of lead soldiers, of the staircase inside the school, of wearing a blue neckerchief and meeting a visiting party dignitary, of playing in the biggest park in Budapest, Városliget (City Park), in the summer with a bicycle, in the winter on a sledge drawn along by my father, of toyshops with magical windows, of piano lessons with my bald tobacco-smelling piano teacher, of visits to one or other parental friend's dacha, of listening to the 1952 Olympic Games on the radio, of being taken to my first football match by my father, of my first terrified reading about the Ku Klux Klan, of my brother's pram, of the night he stuck a knitting needle in my ear while playing, of the sound of fighting outside, of the dull blow on my wrist when a ricocheting bullet struck my toy watch, of early toys, of blue buses with long clumsy noses, of noisy trams, of the interior of the Music Academy, of the smell of the boy I was supposed to help next to me at my desk at school and of the quite different smell of my elderly great-aunt as I clambered onto her lap.

But this is about my mother, and in so far as she appears in these memories she is a permanent yet flittering presence: she is not what happens but the condition under which things happen.

When I am born in 1948 we are still in the far-flung suburb of

Budapest. My mother has a dog – the white *puli* or sheepdog – that starts biting people. Then the dog is gone. Not from my life but from hers.

Then I am born and time continues to wind backwards.

Having arrived at my first moments of conscious life I too am gone, so will no longer refer to my mother as "my mother". She will be her own name – the name I was unknowingly reaching for when she danced in the snowy street – Magda. Magdalena Nussbächer in full. My father will no longer be "my father" but László or its pet form, Laci. He is László Szirtes when I am born, but a year or two before he is his previous name, László Schwarz. I would not be at all surprised if she initiated the change. It would run true to form. Szirtes was, after all, the name of a handsome well-known actor of the time. Changes of name are so common in Hungary it sometimes seems most people have changed names at one time or another. And not only people but places. Once they had both Hungarian and German names. In the Transylvanian part of old Hungary there were names in Hungarian, German and Romanian. The clutter and confusion of names is like a constant noise in the head.

So my mother disappears through the mirror and re-emerges in another life as herself. From now on it is Magda's story.

TWO

Magda

1

Neither Magda nor László ever discussed the circumstances of my birth with me, I know only that she would have preferred for me to be a girl and that she wasn't supposed to have me at all. The little I learned was from László after her death.

He tells me that it was against medical advice. Her heart isn't strong enough, they tell her – and tell her again before András is born, but that is never going to stop her. They have been married for two years by the time I arrive and have their own place, the one out in the sticks. He is already at the ministry, she in one of her two main jobs, either at Operafotó or at *Esti Budapest*.

I am a risk she has chosen to take. She has taken worse risks (as has he) and has faced death directly. I want a child, she says, and she gets me, the little consolation with the deep voice and fancy waistcoat. It is a pity the dog has to go, a creature that would have been more constantly faithful to her than I turn out to be, but that is the natural order of things.

The natural order of things is that the Budapest she has returned to is still in ruins after the siege and life is far from secure. In 1945 men are still being picked off the street by Russian soldiers for *malenky robot*, "a spot of work" in Russia. Many are never to return. The first wave of Russian occupation is characterised by a high level of lawlessness – rape, killings and theft. Women dress as crones not to appear attractive to occupying soldiers. Magda is a highly attractive woman, not yet twenty-two. Everything smells of death. There is little food and no industry except rebuilding.

Food is actually beginning to trickle in from the countryside, but not enough to satisfy demand. Prices rise steeply so the government decides to print money.

These are the facts. In the post-war chaos before communism, in August 1945, hyper-inflation ensued on a scale never reached even by Germany at the end of the First World War. The national currency was the *pengő*. From July 1945 to January 1946 the currency in circulation increased from 25 billion *pengő* to 1.65 trillion. An item that cost about 400 *pengő* in September 1945 cost a trillion trillion by July 1946. The take-home pay that was worth something in the morning was worthless by the afternoon. People looked to be paid as late as possible, and ideally in equivalents. Someone at work would be sent out last thing to find the price of some necessity, salt for example. Whatever the price of salt was, the wage due was calculated by it. In László's place of work wages were calculated per kilo of fat, at Magda's in bottles of soda water. At the height of inflation prices were rising 150,000 per cent per day. The currency was changed from the *pengő* to the *milpengő* (1 million *pengő*) then the *bilpengő* (1 billion *pengő*), finally being replaced by the *adópengő* (or I.O.U.-inflation *pengő*). In August 1946 the *pengő* was dropped altogether in favour of the *forint*, one *forint* being the equivalent of 400,000 quadrillion *pengő* and life could start again.

Behind the scenes whatever remained of Hungary's frail post-war democracy was being dismantled. Under the pressure of Soviet presence, and Stalin's interest in establishing Hungary as his own domain, old bourgeois and peasant-style politicians faced trumped-up charges and vanished from the scene. People who had been imprisoned and tortured by the Nazis were now imprisoned and tortured by the communists.

But anything is better than the war as far as Magda is concerned and certainly far better than the camps, it's just that there is no safety, no security for anyone. No matter. She is going to have a child, maybe two.

2

It is Friday, February 2, 1946. Magda and László are getting married. They stand outside the Aradi utca registry office in heavy winter coats with twenty-two others. The others include Jancsi Stern and his wife, Marika Varga, Auntie Rózsi, Béla Boschán, Aunt Aranka and Gyuri Varga. The couple are framed by direct family, László's mother Margit, and his brother-in-law, Zoli Safir.

Who are these people in their dark coats? Do they matter to Magda who is standing bareheaded in a dazzling white scarf – the brightest object in the picture – next to László, who is wearing his customary trilby. Her outfit beneath the coat, he told me, was a pair of dark-blue trousers, a blue top, a white blouse and a red scarf. But it might have been a black velvet dress with a white lace collar. He wasn't quite sure. He himself was in the brown suit his mother had salvaged from their bombed flat. In any case, both were in their best.

There is nothing after the ceremony. Not even a meal at a restaurant. The couple return to the flat where his mother has prepared a few sandwiches. There is a weekend at a nearby hotel where they spend Friday and Saturday night, but leave on Sunday because they have to work the next day.

No-one from Magda's family is in the photograph. They have vanished and are presumed dead. She knows that. She has tried and failed to find them.

3

Inflation is still raging that summer when Magda falls seriously ill. She simply collapses. Circumstances at home – and home meant at László's mother's flat – have become intolerable as far as she is concerned. Magda's first need is to be loved, but she isn't, she feels. Not by his sister Lili, and clearly not by Margit, his mother. They treat her like an intruder, she says to László who is, after all, his mother's surviving son.

If she loves you so much, how come you were brought up by your aunts, she argues. But my family lived in a tiny flat and there was no room, pleads László. It cuts no ice with her. Margit can't have been loving. She resents and rejects Magda. Has László ever noticed that his mother always gives the best cut of meat to him and the worst to her? Does he know his mother sometimes locks the scullery door to keep her out of it?

There is, he admits, some truth in this. But surely things aren't so bad. Not all the time. Isn't his mother just a Yiddisher momma who, having lost one son to an accident in his infancy, is simply delighted her remaining son has returned from the war in one piece? Her husband, his father, the unsung socialist playwright of the shoe-factory floor, that humble and frustrated man, hasn't returned from Auschwitz and he never will, he tells her. People don't. Perhaps Margit is foolishly hoping her son will stay with her for longer. Perhaps she had hoped he wouldn't get married so soon. All this will pass. They'll have a place of their own. It won't be long now.

Magda has no home to go back to. No mother, no father, no brother. Nobody.

It is a small flat and very crowded. Beside Margit there is not only his sister, Lili, but her baby, Judit. When Magda returns from the camps in May 1945 she has nowhere else to go. Then Lili's husband, Zoli, returns from the war. There is no question before the wedding of László and Magda sleeping in the same room, so Lili, Zoli and baby have one room, László shares a room with his mother, and Magda has the small room to herself. Then Magda decides to sleep at László's aunts' flat. Then Lili and Zoli and baby leave to set up house in Zoli's home town in the Tokay region, where they establish a photography business. (Photography runs right through Magda's life. It is how she met my father.) Then Magda moves back.

Maybe there was no alternative. But it was so predictable. You can see what was bound to happen even in the friendliest and warmest of modern family circles. People see all too much of each other. There is just the one radio for entertainment, the rest is talking or, rather, arguing. People rarely go out since there is little to go out to, and besides, they don't have the money. Minor offences assume vast importance. A glass returned to the wrong place can be the occasion of a furious row. It has got worse since the wedding.

But this isn't the friendliest and warmest of modern family circles. There is more to it than overcrowding.

4

Magda has to take a break from work during her illness, but since staying at home under the circumstances is becoming impossible, László packs what suits he has into a case and goes to a village within easy reach of Budapest. He wants something tranquil, a spare room somewhere, just for a week. He finds one in a peasant's cottage. Because inflation is still inflating the man won't accept money, which is pretty much as László has anticipated, so he offers the man one of his suits. This works. He takes Magda down to the cottage and there she recovers. The trouble is they have to return, but soon it is August and, though they don't yet know it, hyper-inflation is about to end.

This is before the beginning of his political career. He is still working for his pre-war employer Béla Boschán as plumber's mate-cum-bookkeeper. On his return from labour camp, even before their marriage, he, like Magda, had joined the Social

Democratic Party, a party well to the left of centre then, but now about to be absorbed into the Communist Party. He, as we know, is accepted into the new party: Magda is not.

Once she is back at work she is not faced with the prospect of spending whole days in the flat but then, in the spring of 1948, she falls pregnant and she is back there. She grows ever more nervous and irritable so it becomes necessary to move. But where?

In 1947 they had managed a week's holiday at a little half-house in Mátyásföld, an outlying suburb an hour from Budapest by train. In June or July 1948, some four months before I am born, they rent it for a longer term. It consists of one room, a kitchen, a verandah and a bathroom. At about this time Magda's close friend Irén gives them a dog. Magda calls it Mackó, or Bear, which is what she calls László. Magda soon grows to dote on it. Just down the road in Mátyásföld lives a gypsy woman who is reputed to be able to forecast the sex of a baby. Magda crosses the woman's palm with silver. My father is told to drop his handkerchief and she is

asked to pick it up. It will be a boy, says the gypsy woman. How do you know, they ask her? It was the way you picked up the handkerchief, says the woman. Magda is disappointed. She wants a girl. The gypsy woman apologises.

Meanwhile life is rapidly changing. The press becomes ever more an organ of the Communist Party. There are arrests and disappearances. There are new political prisons. There is the split with Tito's Yugoslavia and all the turmoil that brings in its wake. The country is preparing to become a one-party state.

I am born into this, in a small unhygienic clinic where I develop a troublesome rash. Magda is entitled to six weeks paid leave. By now they have found the small shared flat in Budapest so my father can walk to work, first to his old employer, Béla, then, after nationalisation, to his new office in his new job at the ministry. Then comes the move to the beautiful flat with Uncle Sándor's reclaimed baby grand, with the vitrine, the intarsia table, the sideboard, the telephone and Nana Éva.

5

It would be a mistake to think László less interesting than Magda, but this is her story rather than his. Nevertheless, episodes from his life are important since her own would have been different without them. His lightning-fast elevation from the plumbing firm to a high post in the ministry is evidence of something rather extraordinary beyond a talent for administration. He regarded himself primarily as a normal orderly man who could think clearly and organise matters that involved both people and materials. The promotion of his talent to a national scale is astonishing proof of that. But he becomes mysterious in the process. We, as children, had no insight into the world of his work and neither did Magda, except for what he told her: all she saw was how the work affected him.

A senior post in a Moscow-led dictatorship, as Hungary became after 1949, is a different matter. László had to operate under conditions of state paranoia, in an air of mistrust, with the constant suspicion of sabotage, with the threat of arbitrary arrest, and with the murmured resentment of a recently anti-Semitic nation that only five years before had deported more than 400,000 Jews to Auschwitz, at having Jewish upstarts in high office.

In other words László's position was far from secure. The end of the war had brought relief, but not security. Between the wars Jews had kept their heads down: now they were raising them above the parapet. They did not do so officially as Jews – my father had changed his name, as a great many did, precisely to avoid being identified as such – but as atheist or agnostic socialists. Ideology trumped religion. Anti-Semitic remarks were whispered not spoken, but prisons were still full of those who had served fascism. Directors and managers grumbled more than ever about the pervasiveness of "Jewish" power and influence, meaning László among others. Three of the six sections at the ministry were, as we know, run by Jews. The complaints were muted and there was no possibility, not yet, of them being voiced directly – after all, the staff had been hand-picked by the ministry. The dictator himself was Jewish, as were his chief henchmen. This was supposedly a secret, but many knew it.

Magda was not in high office. She met his colleagues, she met party officials, but she did not work where he did. She saw his delight in his elevation, his pride at being, for the first time in his life, an important man in a position of authority, but she also saw and understood his fear. He had changed. In her opinion he was in danger of becoming someone different from the man she had married, the man who was the father of her first child. He was, she thought, a low-level public figure, somewhat intoxicated by power, a little puffed up, like certain others amongst his new colleagues. She was less sure of him. What she did know was that he loved her. Of that, if nothing else, she could be certain.

6

László's two elderly aunts were a great comfort to her. They had brought him up when he was a child, had visited them out in Mátyásföld and had their own flat now close to theirs. They saw each other every week.

Riza was born in 1884, Tini a little later as the youngest of five, though as an adult she looked older than her years. Tini hobbled, liked shopping and would return each day with a jug of milk. László had slept in the same room as his aunts as a child, the other room in the flat being occupied by his grandparents. The aunts slept on a double divan, my father on a single one. There was, apart from that, only a kitchen and bathroom.

The two had sacrificed their lives to their parents. Riza had been a very attractive young woman and had had a fiancé, an officer, who died in the First World War. She had a trousseau full of the usual items – tablecloths, napkins and bedding – things that disappeared piece by piece once the Depression set in. Riza might have fallen in love again, probably with her employer, though that was kept a secret. She was working from home as a seamstress for a fashion house whose owner was a widower. Tini never looked as though she would get married. She was always in the kitchen, always about her chores. Sometimes, when they could afford it, they enjoyed an operetta in town. It was they who had first taken Magda in during the war when László was recalled to the work brigade. Magda regarded them as angels. There were so few angels in life.

7

László was not the first man to propose to her. Before him came George.

George was a slim, handsome captain of the 76th Division in the Third U.S. Army that had fought in the Battle of the Bulge in December 1944 and relieved Penig on April 15, 1945. Penig, about thirty miles south-east of Leipzig, was a work camp for Hungarian women from a cultured background – doctors, artists, musicians, scholars, even photographers – rather than a death camp, though the eventual results were much the same and intended to be so. It was staffed mostly by female guards who administered frequent and severe beatings.

How did she get there in the first place? How was she removed from Hungary? Let me now continue backwards in time and take her back to Budapest and Ravensbrück. Here is her notional voice:

> They put me on a train, east, west or south
> And we rode off in our different directions,
> Myself, my body and my heart. My eyes
> Were saying something to my open mouth
> Which had remained open in surprise,
> And every passenger had his own questions:

My nose asked, what's the smell?
My fingers wondered at the touch of cold,
My hair was busy interrogating the wind.
We were all agog to know the world at last
As it knew itself but never before had told
Anyone. Nor did I mind
Whether this was heaven, earth or hell

As long as we were moving through the air,
As long as the city barked its orders out
Through doorways I imagined everywhere
And heard the porters shout
Behind closed eyes and behind the narrow wall
Of my most valued multi-storeyed skull.

But they told me no great truth, or if they did
I have forgotten it. It was long ago
And I have doubts whether such a truth
Exists at all as something we might know
Or understand. I have my hatred,
Which is proof that something happened in my youth,
And the house itself has not yet been blown down.

My body is still standing. The wind blows through it
Like a language of which not a word
Is what it seems, and yet it survives.
The train is rushing past the fields and woods
Of all that was. The words renew it,
Rephrase its truths and falsehoods.
Behind the thinnest of walls a city thrives,

The empty buildings, the unfurnished
Whose history remains unfinished . . .

In 1986 I published a long poem, “Metro”, in parts of which I tried to speak in the imagined voice of my imagined mother as heard at the moment of her deportation from Budapest. The voice is laid out over the voice map of Budapest, as if the two were aspects of the same identity. Budapest was the maternal city. It was ten years after her death when I wrote it and I myself had just rediscovered the place. My mother and Budapest seemed to contain each other.

It was in some ways a monstrous thing to do and I feared what my real, living father would say. He was not a reader of poetry in English and I doubt he often read mine, but this time he did although his own presence in the poem was almost incidental. The poem was about her, not him. So did he recognise the fictive creature I had created? What was the experience of reading it for him? “It is like walking about inside her,” he said. It was his one and only literary judgment on my work, an astonishingly metaphorical response from someone I had regarded as the epitome of matter-of-fact realism. Without consciously knowing it, that was the response I most craved.

The poem stopped dead at the gates of Ravensbrück. Having trespassed so far I did not feel entitled to go in. I could imagine being taken away all of a sudden. I could imagine a journey. I was caught up in the act of imagining her but my imagination had no right to venture into the camp itself.

8

The distance from Budapest to Ravensbrück, some sixty miles north of Berlin, is almost exactly six hundred miles. (Today it is just over nine hours by car.) Ravensbrück was one of the last camps to be relieved and it was the Red Army that relieved it. The camp, which had been set up in May 1939, was specifically for women but not specifically for Jews, who accounted for only 10 per cent of the prisoners. It was first settled with some 2,000 German prisoners, then expanded to include communists, Jehovah's Witnesses, prostitutes, criminals and Roma, the population rising to a limit of 45,000 at any one time with some 130,000 women passing through it, a good many of those dying there of disease, starvation, overwork and despair – and by being gassed. It is hard to know very much for certain because a great deal of the evidence was destroyed at the time and after.

This combination of prisoners enabled Magda to maintain the fiction that she was sent there for political reasons. This might not have been entirely false since her post-war political instincts were clearly socialist. It might even have been true, as many things might be true in one way or another, but that was not the reason. According to the fiction she was not Jewish at all, or that was the story she told us later, having survived first Ravensbrück then Penig. Madness may entail believing your own fictions, but I don't think she believed them. There were reasons for the fiction. We, her children, were that reason.

And the reason lies partly in Ravensbrück itself.

After days of travel by rail she would have fallen out of the overcrowded cattle wagon to be greeted by dogs on leashes, screams and lashing, and been herded with the others into a great tent. That was because by that time Ravensbrück was already full.

According to one witness, presumably a fellow passenger on the train, there were some 1,500 women and children in the tent at the same time. They were pushed into one half of the tent so that bunks could be constructed in the other half. That took three days. All that time the women were standing, packed very close together and had to remain so throughout the construction. They slept standing, swaying a little, say accounts. László's cousin, Klári, was with her. Klári was five years older than her and would die in Ravensbrück.

There were originally two prisoners per bunk, but some half-starved Poles arrived and then there were three. The clothes they received were of summer weight, their shoes were made of wood. Their hair was shaved off, not just from their heads but from their bodies. They laughed at each other at first. They were served coffee containing bromide. Everyone's periods immediately stopped. There were no toilets, only a bucket at the end of each row of bunks. Once it had been filled, the last to use it had to empty it out. Cigarettes became a vital necessity: people exchanged bread rations for them.

Then there was work, mostly meaningless work. The prisoners dug ditches, carried the earth from one place to another then carried it back again and dug more ditches. The worst thing was the morning parade, the *Appell*, lining up for hours in the cold and dark as winter approached.

There are stories of a column of choking blue smoke. Of the camp hospital where syphilis germs were injected into the spinal cord. Of women arriving on a death march from Auschwitz in heavy snow. Of women from the camp being forced to work in a Dachau brothel. Many had been raped, many more would be. Many had seen their daughters or mothers raped.

I admit to having speculated on her treatment at Ravensbrück.

The guards were mostly female, but there might have been occasions when male guards or visiting officers were allowed to have their way with the prettier women. There was a smaller men's camp nearby. And there was that Dachau brothel as an example.

And then there were the "asocials" who found solace in sex and were evidently no good at keeping their love-making quiet. Other prisoners often spoke of beds shaking and even collapsing in the night. And as lesbianism was a crime within the camp (though not outside), many were caught and thrown into the Strafblock where, as one prisoner Bertha Teege put it, "sexual aberrations got out of hand".

How lurid this is. There are so many places we should not go in the imagination and the sexual life of our parents is one of them. It is, or should be, a side issue. Except it isn't: it never is. It is a part of understanding, or at least of fabricating an understanding one might believe in.

I know she hated to be seen naked, even by László in their bedroom. I have already spoken about her affected brazenness. She referred to the pubic hair no-one ever saw as Acker Bilk, after the beard of the popular clarinettist. She liked the joke, but did she like the thing? Was she just flirting with direct sexuality, suppressing it through flirtation?

She never spoke of sex in terms that reflected her own experience, but there were many other cruelties and deprivations of which she never spoke. The company of the other prisoners would have been something of a consolation at times because they were an elite group of female intelligentsia, artists, philosophers, psychologists, heroes, agents of all nationalities. At different times they included people like Geneviève de Gaulle (General de Gaulle's niece), Violette Szabó and the Czech writer Milena Jesenska, Kafka's correspondent.

Overall there were some 8,000 French, 1,000 Dutch, 18,000 Russians and 40,000 Poles as well as British and Hungarians. Different groups had to wear different shapes and colours of patches. Since she never talked about it in any detail we never knew what shape or colour of patch Magda wore.

How did Magda survive when people were dying all around her, two or three each week in her compound? It was her willpower, according to László. Her will was superhuman. She no longer suffered anxiety. She kept her self-respect. She did not steal or protect herself at all costs. Psychologically she defeated her jailers. Or so he suggests, or so she suggested to him.

So the suggestion passes down to me. Imagined terrors are in the imagination. They can spill over into dreams and nightmares or find form eventually in a narrative of some sort where events come together. There they are safe.

9

In January 1945, some seven hundred Hungarian women aged between thirteen and fifty-one were chosen from amongst those still fit at Ravensbrück to be transferred to Penig, one of more than a hundred sub-camps of Buchenwald and built specially to serve the Max Gehr aeroplane factory that was badly understaffed in the latter stages of the war, all the men having been called into service at the front. There was an urgent need for aeroplane parts and the factory had to be in production twenty-four hours a day, seven days a week.

Plans for the camp had been made in August 1944. It would follow the standard sub-camp model of six to eight huts of standard size, sleeping prisoners in the now-standard three tiers, along with a hut for the S.S. and local guards (the majority of them female), a sick bay, an electric fence and a watch tower. All this had to be situated some distance from the town and away from the main road, ostensibly to avoid notice. A clearing in a wood a few miles down the highway was ideal. The camp construction began at the end of 1944, just at the time when the first female prisoners were being deported from Budapest to Ravensbrück.

Penig was opened on January 9. The women arrived the following day, joined just over a week later by three local Jewish prisoners, two nurses and a dentist.

On arrival the women were showered, then paraded before the female commander who immediately picked out a pretty dancer called Kitty, dressed her in fine clothes and more or less adopted her. Then there was a parade, after which the women were given new summer-weight clothes and equipped with a pair of wooden shoes. No socks, stockings or even handkerchiefs. Then they were organised into shifts and set to work in the factory. The work consisted of three eight-hour shifts, one from 6 a.m. to 2 p.m., one from 2 p.m. to 10 p.m. and one from 10 p.m. to 6 a.m. The shifts began after an hour's march to work, and at the end of the day the march back was much harder, partly because of fatigue and partly because much of it was uphill. The women marched slowly in ranks of five, always changing the order so whoever was in the middle could sleep and be supported by the others. It was January. They were cold and developed blisters on their feet. Their feet bled. They were exhausted, diseased, and lice-ridden. They washed and ate at the factory as and when they could, not in the camp. There was no break.

Even so, Penig was the easier of the two camps. At least there were no crematoria or gas chambers there, only work, starvation and disease.

Magda endured three months of this but she was already exhausted before she came. She was only just twenty-one and had a heart condition. The fierce spirit that kept her alive in Ravensbrück did not fail her in Penig. Her few accounts to us were about bleeding feet and the cold. She said nothing about the sick bay. Nothing about day-to-day life. Nothing about lice.

For those in town or travelling in 1945 it must have been a disturbing sight, ranks of more than two hundred ill-clad, starving women marching past, but few recall it or were willing to recall it. With the customary efficiency a daily count was kept of those fit to work and those being treated in the sick bay. Many more than a hundred were too ill to work on some days. Magda was among them.

She was one of some eighty women left in the sick bay when the others were sent on a death march to Theresienstadt on April 13, 1945. American forces were at the gate and had in fact taken an aerial photograph of the camp that very day. Those who were marched off escaped or died or reached their destination. The situation was chaotic by then. Guards leapt off cars and motorbikes and mixed with prisoners so they should not be bombed. The nearby city of Chemnitz had been reduced to rubble and there was scarcely anything to eat there. Those left behind in the sick bay had nothing at all. They were left without provisions for two days until the Americans arrived on April 15. For those who survived there was the hospital at Altenburg. Then, for Magda, came George.

As she told it to László, it was simply early April, no dates. There was a lot of screaming and no work. Everyone knew the Americans were coming. Those who were fit were lined up by their guards and marched away. American bombers were flying overhead. The Germans were gone. Then the Americans, George among them, arrived.

When Magda was rescued she weighed only thirty-eight kilos: six stone.

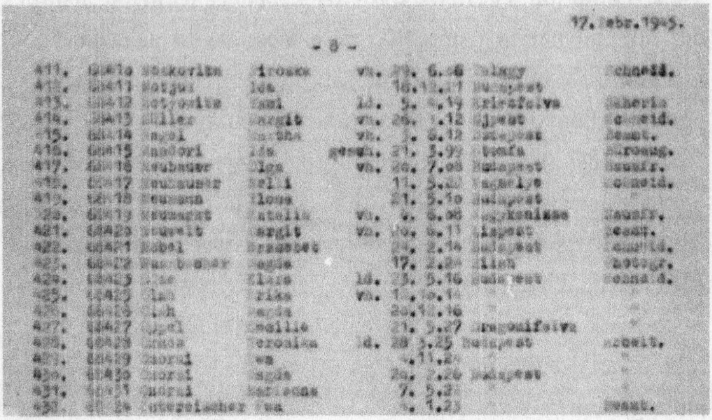

10

There is a U.S.-army film, now readily available on the net, of the liberation of Penig. It shows the inside of the sick bay. It concentrates on a few women. Some are in terrible shape, quite skeletal and hardly able to stand. Others have rashes and lacerations. The film shows some of them naked from the waist down to display their skeletal legs and their sores. Their faces are intelligent, wild-eyed, exhausted. They are all at one or other stage of starvation, suffering from fever, tuberculosis, typhoid and gangrene. Some of them did not survive long beyond their liberation.

The film goes on to show them being carried on stretchers to the nearby Luftwaffe hospital where the German nurses are made to care for them. You see some of them in the hospital, recovering.

Not all. I have searched this film several times hoping to find an image of Magda, but either she is unrecognisable (she could be this or that fleeting face) or was simply not in shot.

In any case she was nursed back to health. After a month or so she was as before, the figure trim and natural, the face full of life.

That was where George fell for her. A photograph shows them together in the covered porch of the hospital on a fine spring day under an external night light. I recognise it from the film. He cannot be tall since she was about 5′1″ and he is only four or five inches taller. He is bare-headed with neat glossy hair. There is a touch of the young Errol Flynn or Ronald Colman about him. His moustache makes him look older than he is but even so he can't be more than thirty. His arm is around her shoulders, hers around his waist, her hand resting on his wrist. She leans in to him, relaxed in her matching two-piece light-coloured outfit comprised of a pleated skirt and a little jacket with three big buttons on the front. It fits her perfectly She has no jewellery but is wearing medium heels. She is the fashionable young woman I never met. It is, I suspect, more than a souvenir photograph taken by an unnamed photographer: it is something a soldier might send home to show his mother, as if to say, see, this is the girl. Somebody else was taking it, obviously. He would have asked a friend. There would have to have been time for someone to develop and print it because he gave her a copy for her to keep. It was to remind her of him.

How did she come by the outfit? An outfit she was still wearing after her marriage, as the later photograph shows. Magda would have had nothing but what she stood up in in the camp. It is unlikely to have been lying around. According to László, George's mother sent it. George must have written home with the right measurements and his mother must have dispatched the clothes pretty quickly since Magda was not going to be there very long.

It is difficult to imagine those few months straight after liberation. I know she is a younger version of the woman I saw dancing in the snow. I can even associate her starved look at the point George found her in her condition near the end of her life, but it would be an insult to her to guess the state of her heart and mind or to gauge her feelings for George. I like him, the little I know of him. I assume he survived the war and went home to his mother and waited for a letter. His mother would have asked him about the clothes. Did they fit? How did she look in them? And he would have produced the photograph and said: Like this. And what was she really like? his mother would want to know. As do I.

George wanted her to go to America with him, but she asked him to wait. She desperately wanted to find her family in

Transylvania first. In any case she was already engaged to László. She said she would write to George once she knew about her family. I expect she kept her word. She always did.

In the end she chose to remain in Hungary with László. Nevertheless she must have been very fond of George because when I was born she gave me the Hungarian equivalent of his for my middle name.

My father certainly knew about American George, but the Hungarian equivalent, György, is common enough and does not immediately conjure the English name. Besides, as my mother confessed one time, she was so keen on girls that she hadn't thought of any boys' names, so when the registrar called to ask what I should be called, she rattled off three names: Gábor. György. Miklós. She said she was just trying them out for size but the registrar wrote them all down in that order and the matter was settled. It was settled for my father, too. He was assured of her love. She needed him and American George was gone, probably for ever.

11

Anyone who has read Primo Levi's *The Truce* will know that returning home was not a simple matter. He tells the story over two hundred pages since the route of his journey is perversely long. It took him thirty-five days and was never less than dangerous, but at least when he got home his house was still standing and all of his family were still alive.

Magda's journey did not take as long, but was no less fraught. After a little over a month in the hospital she was given the option of joining an eastbound train going ultimately to Belgrade. On board were a number of Italian and Yugoslav liberated prisoners of war. Railways had been a primary target for allied bombing so the route would have been tortuous, neither track nor rolling stock anywhere near pre-war condition. As it happens this was a goods train due to call at Budapest. She had been on worse. She was wearing some of the clothes George had given her and had two friends from Penig for company, Vilma – a needy woman with whom she kept in contact even after coming to England – and a young woman they called Egérke or Little Mouse. There would have been plenty of others from Penig, but the passengers were mostly male. The train was passing through Russian-occupied territory when some drunken Russian soldiers attempted to take the women off the train but the Italians and Yugoslavs resisted. The Russians fired a few rounds into the air but let them go.

I know this from László's account since there is no other record of Magda's journey – so much is fragmentary – but assuming the train started in Leipzig it presumably passed through Chemnitz, Prague, Brno and Bratislava, or it would today. There is no guarantee it did then. The alternative major route was through Nuremberg, Passau and Vienna. There would have been delays and detours and the route lay through ruins in a war-torn landscape.

She arrived in Budapest in late May, then had to find László's new address because his old block of flats no longer existed.

László had arrived some months earlier on the back of a Red Army truck. He had escaped from the route march back from Belarus as it passed through Hungary and had hidden on a farm with a couple of friends. His experience of the war was of labour camps behind the Russian front and he was one of the relatively few survivors of the harsh life. His first sight of the Russians was of figures pouring over the hill in no distinct formation, both men and women, some in uniform, some without, some with regulation arms, some with whatever they could get hold of. He was picked up along the way and dispatched from post to post, narrowly avoiding deportation to Siberia, before being offered the opportunity to return to Budapest on that military truck.

He returned home to discover his block badly damaged and uninhabitable but he located his family by asking around. They had moved in elsewhere, having escaped deportation by taking shelter in a protected house. Not that the protection was foolproof by the time of the siege, as Magda had already found out.

On May 26 or 27, László had been out at work and had just arrived home when he heard shouting downstairs. She is back! Magda is back! And there she was, coming up the stairs in a dark-blue skiing outfit with a rucksack on her back.

12

I rarely heard her speak about her family, but I do know her first thought was to locate them back in Kolozsvár. Since at the time there was no way of getting there by train, she prepared to walk. For once László persuaded her against it. It would have been far too dangerous, he argued. And indeed it would have entailed a journey of almost three hundred miles across Russian-occupied territory, particularly hazardous for a young woman travelling alone.

She had to wait until September to get a train. She was already back at work by that time but asked for two weeks' leave and set off as soon as she could. It was a fruitless journey. Neighbours told her all the Jews had been taken away. Someone said her brother had been in a labour camp. Someone else told her that he had been murdered by the Germans, or whoever was guarding him, near the Russian border as the Red Army advanced. There was no precise information but she knew that he had been a socialist, so imagined that he might have died fighting in the resistance. She certainly liked to think so, and it was what she told us.

Before they were deported her parents had written to tell her that, in case anything should happen to them, they had buried their valuables in the garden. Whatever they buried was gone by September 1945. Neighbours mentioned someone who might have been responsible for digging the things up, but the man was nowhere to be found. Worse still, some of the nearest neighbours, Hungarian neighbours, didn't seem to care. They hadn't objected to the removal of the Jews and didn't want to speak to her. This rejection, one of many, was to colour her view of Hungarians for the rest of her life.

Magda had been fundamentally altered by her experience of Ravensbrück and Penig, and the visit to Kolozsvár compounded the change which was gradual but clear. She grew bitter about humanity at large. She didn't trust women any more than she did men. After all, her guards at both Ravensbrück and Penig had been female and were as savage as any man could be. People had to earn her trust and once they earned it they had to be careful never to betray it, although, as time went on, they might betray it without ever knowing they were doing so.

Magda had survived three months in Penig and two in Ravensbrück and yet within a couple of years produced me. At one point, like many others, she passed through death and entered the zone of survival.

I cannot explain Magda by Ravensbrück or Penig. I cannot define her in such exclusive terms. She had had twenty years of life before and had thirty years after. However terrible the experience of the camps they weren't the only events of her life, nor indeed of any other survivor's life. In each case it was a whole person who went in and a whole person who came out, it's just that the relation between the two had changed. Magda's real bitterness, László noted, was not evident in the immediate aftermath of the camps but followed the discovery that all her family had perished and that their perishing was greeted with either indifference or pleasure by those who had previously seemed good-natured and neighbourly.

It would have taken prodigious will and concentration on Magda's part to keep going through the various crises of the camps. Each effort would be followed by exhaustion, then more work, more suffering and another crisis. Little by little the relief provided by thoughts of the past, of others, of those loved, of stories or songs or jokes, fades away. Then comes the sick bay, the hovering between life and death in a state of starved semi-consciousness. Then the slide towards death that does not come.

Everyone leaves. You are starving. The dying around you continue to die. The Americans arrive. There is the sensation of being lifted up, of being prodded and looked at, of being carried by truck to a hospital, of being lowered onto a clean bed – a proper bed! – then medical examinations, more careful, more human, the voices quieter, the light sweeter, the sign of ever-more-healthy bodies moving around a ward, the dawning to consciousness of spring, to breeze and warmth and scent. There is food, a carefully gradated increase in diet, the return of taste and smell. The touch and feel of knife and fork and spoon and plate. The relative softness of cloth, the simple cleanliness, followed by the slow rediscovery of the body as pleasure, the rediscovery of the autonomy of one's own self. Look! Dark hair, an emaciated face beginning to fill out, a body regaining its shape, the sense of being a woman in a world of women and men, no longer a walking corpse. There are unfamiliar voices, a strange language, a dramatic change in the manners of other people entailing the recovery and partial repossession of a social status that comradeship in suffering has modified so that the relationship between professor and street-cleaner is never quite the same again.

After the sudden end to suffering there is the numbness, the haze of recovery, that suspension of time between events when you know next to nothing of one moment's relationship to another, when it's all present tense, a succession of present tenses without context. Then there is George's proposal of marriage and the arrival of dresses from America.

I am inventing her again, but only to a degree. What I imagine here is not specific to her, it is only a guess, possibly a wrong one, about the process of recovery in general, albeit in a specific place, in Altenburg, Middle Saxony, spring 1945. It is an invention I can justify only by claiming that any knowledge is partly invention, that memory is mostly invention, and that knowledge of another is invention in the highest degree. Then I must go on to claim that invention can be a form of love. We address our human inventions with the same solicitude with which we address any other of our own inventions. We even invent ourselves, though with far less security. We keep inventing and inventing, growing tired of our inventions. We should reinvent ourselves occasionally, we think, sometimes even drastically. But in doing so we destroy other people's inventions of us. We have to invent everything all over again and so do they. That is a serious responsibility.

I am interested in her so I go on inventing her, inventing a truth I can believe in. I invent nothing factual. I don't make it up, but the person at the core of it all still has to be constructed and understood in terms of invention.

The trick is to invent the truth.

13

Magda had met László during the war when he was home on leave from labour camp. Those who worked in such camps were officially part of the army and so received occasional leave. His sister Lili, who, like Magda, worked at a photographer's studio, was out when Magda called round with a box of negatives. He invited her to wait. They talked for a while then she had to go, so he escorted her down the three floors and they decided to keep in touch. It was a simple matter, something as simple as this, the poem "Meeting 1944", spoken in László's voice:

I opened the front door and stood
lost in admiration of
a girl holding a paper box
and that is how we fell in love.

I've come, she said, to bring you this,
some work from the photographer,
or rather it's for a Miss D –
would you pass it on to her?

She's my sister, but she's out.
You must wait for her inside.
I'm expecting her right now.
Come in. I held the front door wide.

They talk and he sees her down the stairs, then adds:

I think they were such simple times
we died among simplicities,

and all that chaos seemed to prove
is what a simple world it is

that lets in someone at the door
and sees a pair of lives go down
high hollow stairs into the rain
that's falling softly on the town.

That would have been before the Germans marched in, early in 1944, and Eichmann set about his lethal task. He began by emptying out the provinces, including the northern part of Transylvania where Magda's family lived (an area again under Hungarian control since 1940), then, later in the year, made a start on Budapest.

How did she come to be living with his family? It may be that in the course of conversation she said something about needing somewhere new to live and that he offered her a room, possibly his sister's – since she was living between apartments at the time – possibly his own. He would be away, of course. That may be how it happened. He didn't say. The fact remains that some time after the German occupation, after he left, she moved in and was living there. She and László were an item by then. I know that because one of his most vivid memories was of the pair of them sitting in a Budapest café watching the arrival of the Germans on March 19.

László returned to Ukraine to live his own endangered life of forced labour, to avoid freezing or working himself to death, to chop trees, to retreat before the advancing Russian army, to escape on the march back, and then, having earlier seen the arrival of the German army, to find himself in a farmhouse from which he could observe the arrival of the Russians and compare the orderliness of the former with the apparent randomness of the latter.

For all the dangers László faced it was better to be out of the way than in Budapest. By the end of June some 435,000 of 700,000 Jews had been deported, the majority of them to Auschwitz.

Deportations from Budapest began in October and continued into February though the Russians were at the gates and inside the city by January 17. Despite this, the Arrow Cross, the Hungarian Nazi militia, seemed more keen to rid the world of Jews than to save the country. On November 29, 1944, they set up a walled ghetto, exactly like those in other Nazi-occupied European cities, that is to say without egress, without food, without waste collection, the dead piled in the street and typhoid rampant, in the old Jewish district just behind the great Dohány utca synagogue. They conducted impromptu executions of up to 20,000 Jews on the banks of the Danube and rushed others to concentration and death camps.

Not all Jews were in the ghetto though. Special visas, letters of conduct and safe passage vouchers were quickly arranged by individual diplomats of various countries often acting against the instructions of their own governments – the British, the Americans, the Chinese, the Portuguese, even the Vatican and the Japanese, but above all by the Swiss, represented by Carl Lutz, and by the Swedes, represented by Raoul Wallenberg who, between them, set up dozens of diplomatically protected houses in Budapest although those houses would not necessarily remain safe, not all the time, and Wallenberg himself was to be arrested on January 17 by the Russians, never to reappear.

Somewhere in Pest, not far from the Seventh District, is the fourth-floor flat in the tenement block where László's mother and sister, the sister's baby and Magda are huddled. There is a curfew on Jews, so when Magda goes out to shop she has to watch the time carefully.

14

One day in late November or early December Magda comes home, but no sooner is she inside the gate of the block than she is aware of an Arrow Cross group close behind her, moving along the street. She rushes up to the fourth floor, opens the door and calls out the names of her future mother-in-law and sister-in-law, but they . . .

This is where accounts vary.

Magda's account says that they fail to answer her. They have hidden somewhere and will not reveal themselves. She is stung by this betrayal. It means they don't care for her. Maybe they don't want her with them at all. Very well, then, she won't bother them anymore, so she deliberately steps out of the apartment to the gangway that runs right round the open courtyard and makes herself visible. The Arrow Cross are in the courtyard now, see her and order her down. And she goes. And that is the beginning of Ravensbrück and Penig, with a betrayal and the decision to step through a door.

This is her imagined voice in "Metro".

I was on the fourth floor when the yard
Filled with uniforms and we were called
To order, and I ran into the flat we shared,
The old woman, her daughter and the child,
And all was empty. I whispered their names,
But they did not answer to their lasting shame.
They should have answered me out of the pit,
Like any prompter from his own hell-hole,
But they closed their mouths to my pitiful dole
So I went down and here's the end of it . . .

Many years later, some twenty years after Magda dies, the sister and the child in the flat come to London to visit László. Magda, being dead, can no longer ban communication between them, not even a visit as brazen as this. I meet them there for the first time. Lili, the sister, is a very sweet elderly figure, full of warmth and affection; her daughter, Judit, an intelligent, friendly blonde woman just a few years older than I am.

László has flown out to see them in Buenos Aires twice after Magda's death, to make up for lost time and to speak to his sister and mother while she is still alive. He has also sent them *Metro*, my latest book. We are walking along the street on the way to a restaurant when Judit falls in with me a little way in front of the others, who move at Lili's slower pace.

It isn't true, she says.

What? I ask.

The story of her arrest. Or at least it didn't happen exactly as she told you.

What did happen?

Not that, she says. They couldn't answer, she adds. They weren't there.

Then we are in the restaurant, spread around the big table and the conversation moves on. It is a social occasion, not a historical review. It is only Judit who refers to this, not Lili. Margit, his mother, has died by now, aged a hundred.

They had left Hungary at the same time as we did in 1956. Margit, still an attractive middle-aged woman, married a wealthy businessman and lived in style for some years, but when he died he cut her out of his Will and she was reduced to poverty. She had to spend her last years being looked after by her daughter in a cramped flat in a poor part of the city. László sent money to support them. When Margit died, Judit, by then divorced and with two children, was left to look after Lili. Life was hard but at least they had survived the war without being deported. Most of their relations, like Magda's, had gone up in smoke.

So much hinges on the moment of Magda's dash into the flat and on her emergence from it. She cannot have had any idea what she was walking out to. Hardly anyone would, or at least it wasn't clear at the time. Even so, the fury that made her turn on her heel and face the Arrow Cross would not have been entirely a new feeling for her. Life was a matter of endless recovery from rejections. This was not her city. This was the city that was rejecting and betraying her. She could say goodbye to it and feel no loss. Who knew what would happen anyway? Perhaps they were all bound to be discovered and punished. László might never come back. She might never see her family again. It was that sort of world, a world that had to be confronted. The confrontation needed energy and rage. She had to be strong and would be stronger than anyone else in the flat, in the building, and in the city if it came to that. She was only twenty and had enough energy and spirit to see it through and if she didn't – well, she could die having at least tried.

So she steps out of the flat into a condition that will last the rest of her life and will cut the ground, or some of it, from under László's feet too.

I am reading this into her. The bullet holes and shell marks on Budapest buildings were her wounds. The blasted statuary that projected from wall after wall was her. She was a piece of broken statuary. I understood this process as I understood her, in other words hardly at all.

15

Magda had resolved to be a photographer when she left school at fourteen and she studied photography for two years in her home city of Cluj, or Kolozsvár, also known as Klausenburg, before taking up the newly available opportunity of continuing her studies in Budapest. That opportunity came about because of the Second Vienna Award of 1940, championed by Hitler and Mussolini, intended to address the grievances of Hungary and to reward the country for joining the Axis powers. The first Vienna Award in 1938 had restored those chunks of Poland and Slovakia that had been part of Hungary before the First World War. The second Vienna Award did the same with Northern Transylvania, including Kolozsvár.

Understanding these changes is important because those same grievances are still central to Hungarian life. The Awards were regarded as restorations because these regions and others had all been part of the Kingdom of Hungary for centuries and had substantial Hungarian populations. The Treaties of Versailles and Trianon had cut off more than two thirds of the map of pre-war Hungary and left roughly a third of Hungarians marooned in hostile territory. Few families were left unaffected by the change.

Trianon was signed in 1920. Had Magda been born five years earlier she would have been a citizen of Hungary, but as things were she was an ethnic Hungarian, yet Romanian by birth. After Vienna she became Hungarian and remained so until the war ended, when both Vienna Awards were scrapped and she was officially Romanian again, albeit a Hungarian-speaking citizen of Hungary.

These changes of status and identity left traces on her already intense emotions. Life was a succession of great ambitions and wild hopes followed by disaster. Her volatility is shared by many contemporary Hungarians, it's just that in her case life, in the form of what was to happen, chose to amplify and confuse it.

Budapest must have been an enormous thrill. Kolozsvár, for all its civility and charm, is a provincial city, more rural than industrial, more York or Norwich than Manchester or Birmingham. Budapest was a European metropolis, its architecture resonant with imperial echoes and a barely disguised, almost vulgar yearning for grandeur. In 1900 it had been the fastest-growing capital in Europe. About a fifth of the country's population lived there. The city could turn your head and dazzle you with its operas, theatres, music halls, zoo, funfair, monuments, underground system and much else. The grand tenements of Pest accommodated both rich landlords and the desperately poor, while the fantastical villas, steep passages, cog-wheel railway, spectacular chair lift and the magical fairy-tale bastion of Buda offered a dream home to the vestigially decadent yet solid bourgeois life carried over from the last days of Franz Joseph. Budapest was by far the biggest city Magda had ever seen and much the most exciting. It also had its Jewish population trying to keep its head down, Hungaricising its Germanic names, and steering clear of politics, the law and everything else.

16

It was in 1983, after the publication of three books of poetry, that I first felt the desire to visit Budapest. I could not proceed either as a writer, even as a man, without understanding a vital part of my own early life. I applied for a grant for the first and only time, got it, and began to read. I read throughout our holiday in Scotland that summer – not books in Hungarian since my own grasp on the language had loosened year by year until it seemed I had lost all contact with it – but *about* Hungary in English. I read histories and whatever literature in translation I could find. I had understood that I could make no further progress in writing unless I returned. Budapest was my subsoil. I had, at the very least, to set foot on it.

For three weeks I wandered around as in a hallucination, meeting parts of myself in buildings and streets that presented an alternative reality. Everything was familiar: nothing was specific. Before 1989 no-one was insured against burglary and the courtyards were still open to any passer-by. I could wander into tenement after tenement and sense the distinction between the private life of flats and corridors and the roar and cries of the street. I could peel the city like an overripe fruit.

Three longer poems resulted from this visit, which in effect changed my life.

The first was about the courtyards themselves, the interior spaces of both physical and mental worlds. It was about their history. So much stucco had fallen outside and in the stairwells, so many statues were broken on the façade. So much had happened here. So much anxiety, fighting, death and survival. Beauty too. I wanted to register the texture of walls, the light on the third, fourth and fifth floors, the sound of steps along the inner corridors, the radios, the clanking of saucepans.

One of Magda's old friends, Rózsi, who had been the plumber Béla's wife but was now widowed, had lost her sight and had to creep along the fourth-floor corridor holding on to the rails. She would lower the key to the lift by feeding it down a long piece of string that was just long enough for us to fit the key into the lock. Her aged brother lived with her. On the shelves and sideboards in the flat were displayed a few small porcelain figures from before the war: coy shepherdesses, bold twisting nudes. The bathroom and kitchen were rudimentary. She asked us to bring instant coffee from England. This was their world and had been Magda's too.

The second poem was entirely about her as a photographer. I watched her touching her skin, checking the camera in its case, getting ready to go out and catching a last glimpse of herself in the mirror before making her way out into the snow. I sat behind her ghost on the tram and trailed her down the street. My ghost addressed and interrogated her ghost. "Where are you going? To work? I'm watching you. / You cannot get away." I got her to pose for me:

> . . . Please
> Co-operate with me and turn your head,
> Smile vacantly as if you were not dead
> But walked through parallel worlds. Now look at me
> As though you really meant it. I think we could be
> Good for each other. Hold it right there. Freeze.

I was David Hemmings in "Blow-Up", bestriding her, turning her own camera on her. I accused her of lying by employing hand-colouring. I watched her work at it. I lost track of who was subject, who object.

> I go on taking pictures all the same.
> I shoot whole rolls of film as they shoot me.
> We go on clicking at the world we see
> Disintegrating at our fingers' ends.

In the third I transferred her to England, not to where she lived but where we did. I imagined the floor of the local church opening up like black ice to reveal the dead swimming in vast shoals beneath. I recalled those who had been shot into the icy Danube in the last months of the war, among them a girl I had read about, who had managed to survive both the guns and the water by swimming to the other shore. But what language did the dead speak down there, under the ice? How did they communicate?

The poem "Metro" with Magda's removal from the city came later, with apocalyptic images of a whole underground city, where passengers waited on underground platforms while individual flames flickered above their heads.

One of my most abiding fantasies was conceived at this time but not written down for another five years. In it Magda returns from work and begins to climb the stairs in one of those decaying, war-damaged tenement buildings that is home to her. The front of the building is decorated with plaster statues, caryatids, allegorical representations and so forth, mostly blown away, missing heads and limbs.

She stops at the door of the flat, takes out her key and lets herself in. She puts down her bag and takes off her coat, but instead of sitting down in a chair she carries on walking through the wall until she emerges as one of the plaster statues. She is broken statuary. At that moment I realise all the statues were tenants once, that Budapest is absolutely crammed with statues that were once people, people who had simply walked through the walls and become stylised allegorical figures, that this was their fate, hers, and mine too, come to that.

17

There is an Ancient Greek figure called a psychopomp, a kind of spirit or angel whose task it is to conduct the living into – and, with luck, through – the land of the dead. Charon and Hermes are such figures and Virgil performs that function for Dante. These creatures can take various forms: deer, dogs, horses, crows, sparrows, owls. They provide safe passage. By 1986 Magda had become my psychopomp in Budapest. She would provide safe passage. She had to. She was, after all, my mother.

Like each great city in its own way, Budapest is a smell. You smell its being as soon as you enter it. It's not like Vienna or Prague or Paris, let alone London. It's not just the buildings, but the scuttle and hurry of it, the noise it makes, the wild gestures combined with the "fuck you, what do I know" shrugs. There are the bitter jokes, the hunched shoulders, the impatient glances of sharp eyes, the learned and cultivated charm, the peculiar squalor of its poverty and the vulgar display of its wealth. For Magda, as she was then, it is 1940. In Budapest there is no war, not yet, but a coldness that has been creeping through the city for twenty years has now reached a critical point. There is ice in the heart and scorn in the eyes.

Magda has to make her way around. There are buses and trams, the relatively new trolleybuses and a single shallow underground line that heads out of the centre towards the park with the zoo and the funfair. You can feel the throb of the trains beneath your feet. You can get cheap rooms in the attics of the big tenements and be in walking distance of pretty well everything of interest.

Importantly for Magda, Budapest is the city of great photographers – mostly Jewish – of André Kertész, Brassaï, László Moholy-Nagy and Marton Munkácsi amongst others who had flown the nest by then, partly to escape the stifling anti-Semitic atmosphere of the city, partly because greater fame and wealth were to be found elsewhere. They left about the time Magda was born, but Károly Escher, as important and gifted as any of them, had not. Magda's mother had accompanied her to Budapest to arrange the final details of an apprenticeship that had already been negotiated. That apprenticeship was to Károly Escher.

This was the beginning of the great age of magazine photography involving the documentation of public events, the exposure of private joys and miseries, the capturing of glamour, the recording of poverty in the Great Depression, the celebration of the advance of science and fashion, and the business of keeping an eye on the growing political unrest in Europe. Escher, who was already fifty by this time, had taken plenty of pictures of the poor and had in fact started as a cinematographer in commercial cinema while at the same time making propaganda films for the short-lived Hungarian Bolshevik Republic of 1919. It has always been important in Hungary to learn the art of survival and Escher must have been particularly good at it. In 1940 he was working as the principal photographer on two major magazines, one of them dedicated to film and theatre. He had the great photographer's instinct for the symbolic subject at the symbolic moment and would have been Magda's ideal master had he been less busy.

It is difficult now to tell what direct influence he exercised on her because so little of her own photographic work remains: there are only her family photographs, which are sometimes beautiful but limited in scope, and not of this period.

18

Modern photography, like Escher's, might have been an escape from the studio, but having a studio was inescapable and she, as an apprentice, must have spent much of her time doing fairly menial tasks while learning skills such as hand-colouring and retouching.

An apprenticeship had to be paid for, so she took on a variety of casual part-time jobs. The only one she talked about with any fondness was modelling jewellery.

Magda had unusually long and flexible fingers. She could bend those fingers back like a Nepalese dancer at what seemed to us as children a terrifying and unnatural angle. It hurt us just to look at it. But they came in useful at the jeweller's where her task was to sit behind velvet curtains in the shop window and display the wares. She would push her hands through curtains and move them in a graceful way while wearing various rings and bracelets, feeding precious necklaces through those extraordinary eye-catching fingers. She was the sole moving exhibit in a static glittering display. No-one else had hands like that. When her nails were painted and sharp she would tease us by pretending they were the claws of a monster. But they were beautiful hands.

The quality that unites beauty and terror was implicit in her very being; it was there in her fingers.

19

Király utca, where Magda was living with two other girls, forms the whole border of the VII District ghetto. For the most part it is a fairly narrow commercial street with a ragbag of nineteenth-century tenements of two to six storeys in a variety of styles – romantic, classical, eclectic, art deco – and in various states of preservation. In 1940 it was festooned with a mass of hanging shop signs advertising the cheaper trades.

Budapest was, and remains, an eminently walkable city and Király utca is close enough to the centre. If you had further to go you could catch one of the overcrowded trams with passengers clinging on, dripping from the carriage like bunches of grapes. Magda's block was only about ten minutes' walk away from where László's family were living. There was no gated ghetto in 1940, but the district was largely Jewish within easy reach of three central synagogues, the one in Dohány utca being the largest in Europe and the second largest in the world.

Did she ever enter them? Her post-war life would suggest she did not. Her own family were secular reform Jews and she herself never evidenced any sign of hankering after Jewish festivals or specifically Jewish company. Furthermore she kept us from them for what now seem obvious reasons.

20

She left school at fourteen, but that wasn't entirely to do with photography. She had contracted rheumatic fever. This meant time out of school, in fact it meant confinement in the house. The house, she once said, was damp, built into a hill, and her bedroom was partly in the earth so she was in effect entombed. It was a townhouse, one of a series of rows overlooking the municipal park where people would skate in the winter. Her school friends skated there too. During her convalescence she could look out of the window and wave to them, but she could not join them. They would see her and wave back.

I looked for this park in 1993 when Clarissa and I first visited Kolozsvár. This was not four years after the fall of Ceauşescu and I had discovered an elderly cousin of Magda's who was still living there. Uncle Feri was about my father's age by then, but his surname, Kardos, was the same as Magda's mother's maiden name. I had learned of his existence through my father. We had thought they were all dead, the Kardoses and all the paternal-side Nussbächers too, but no. Like László, he had survived his stint in forced labour to return to Kolozsvár once all was done. He had attended a Jewish school and, after the war, worked in offices in mid-managerial positions, possibly in some form of engineering in Ceauşescu's Romania, and had then retired. He was about seventy and spoke no English. Now here he was. He was keen to see us.

We had taken a train from Budapest to get there. It was the filthiest train I had ever been on. Everything was covered in grime. The toilet doors were off their hinges or missing altogether. A young woman with immaculately clean clothes sat opposite us, fastidiously reading a history of France. She was the only other person in our compartment. We stopped for a few hours on the Romanian border and soldiers came round to check our luggage and documents. They also removed a young black man, presumably for no other reason than that he was black. After an hour or so they let him back on. The train continued on its way, arriving at Kolozsvár, now strictly to be called by its Romanian name, Cluj, at dusk.

The station smelled strongly of urine. Few got off. Uncle Feri was waiting by the exit. He ushered us into a taxi where he switched to Romanian and said not a word to us in either Hungarian or in the broken English in which he addressed Clarissa. Not allowed, he explained when we arrived at his flat. For many years it had been obligatory to speak only Romanian in public. You had to be careful even in the street. One in every fifteen citizens was either in the state security police or informing for it. You could be arrested and jailed for speaking Hungarian.

Uncle Feri was to play the part of Virgil to my Dante in the long poem, "Transylvana", that appeared in my book *Blind Field* in 1994. This is how he makes his appearance in the poem:

> Our Virgil is thin. He waves a red carnation
> in his outstretched hand. His mouth is sad.
> Urine and darkness. Taxis hover at the station
>
> like flies round rotten fruit. Roads being bad
> we shake and bump along, juddering on scarred
> cobbles, loose flakes of tarmac, past semi-clad
>
> Seventies blocks. The driver brakes hard
> as we shimmy round a tight bend then lets fly.
> Here only patience is its own reward
>
> and patience is unending, numbing, sly,
> deflated, almost anaesthetic in effect,
> sensations slowing up, the batteries dry.

Uncle Feri's flat was in a nineteenth-century building in the town centre. It would have been a desirable residence at some stage but all he had were two bedrooms and a sitting room plus a small kitchen and bathroom. He had little food to offer us and what he had he handled with forensic delicacy. His wife had died, but he had kept all her dresses and shoes neatly lined up in the wardrobe as if she were standing in her own queue. When it started to rain the next day he offered Clarissa his dead wife's shoes. It rained constantly the whole time we were there, which was just four days.

He was a sweet and gentle man, but his mouth was sad and his eyes verged on tears. He could dress quite sharply, but sorrow hung around him like a veil. At the same time he was generous to a fault and introduced us to some fellow Hungarians though he still refused to speak the language in the street in case anyone was following and listening. It was what he was used to.

Uncle Feri had a small library of standard classics as well as a radio and a television, although the television image had a strong blue tint as though the blood had been sucked out of it by some Transylvanian vampire and there was no way to adjust it. He took us for walks around the city, past half-finished blocks of flats, past piles of rubbish in the streets where cars scuttled, their bodywork damaged, the paintwork on them and the local trams applied roughly by hand in an approximation of the original colour. Not only the train but the whole town was filthy. That included a number of citizens. I had never seen so many people with amputated limbs. The river was orange-yellow, the colour of sulphur. There was nothing in the shops which were still lit by low-wattage bulbs. The supermarket had one small piece of cheese on offer, wrapped in cellophane with a large blob of smut inside the wrapping. That, whispered Uncle Feri as we left, is how I judge national culture. In Toronto there were fifty kinds of cheese in the supermarket, in London thirty-nine. This is Romania.

We offered to take him out for a meal or at least treat him to something. He categorically refused. There was nothing to buy and no restaurant that he would trust. Eventually he rang a private house whose garden served as a kind of diner. He asked what the soup was. They told him and he took us down there.

He could not quite recall where Magda's family had lived. He did take us to one park with a small municipal pond that could have been used for skating in the winter, and there was indeed a hill with houses, but he wasn't quite convinced it was the place and, to be frank, nor was I. It was empty and ragged with leaves that had fallen in the hot, dry summer. But it was a candidate, an image one might grasp and explore. It would have to do.

There were rumours of a train strike when we were due to return to Budapest, but we couldn't confirm them. Uncle Feri rang the station time and again, but there was no answer. Eventually we decided to walk there and ask in person. We arrived at a fine building and entered a rather grand hall that had long been neglected. There seemed to be no-one else there. We waited some minutes at the vacant ticket desk that was covered in dust. Then we heard two young women talking to each other at the far end. Uncle Feri walked over and asked them to attend to us. One did. Is there a strike tomorrow? he asked in Romanian. I don't know, said the woman. Ask her what we should do, I urged him. She shrugged. Come down when your train is due and see whether it comes or not. Then she walked back to her colleague.

In the event we did not risk it and booked places on a minibus to Budapest. It was rough and ready and drove through spectacular landscapes, on crumbling roads, past valleys strewn with rubbish, before spending five hours of the night and early dawn waiting at the village border post while a trail of men waving bottles lurched after two young women in hotpants. It seemed to be a regular trade.

I visited Uncle Feri twice more over the years after that first meeting, as circumstances improved. His eyes grew less sorrowful, his clothes almost dapper, then, suddenly, he was dead. The last strand was gone.

21

The beautiful city of Cluj, as Romanians call it, Kolozsvár as Hungarians called and still call it, and Klausenburg as it was referred to in the Austro-Hungarian period, had not always been like this. Not in Magda's time. If from now on I call it by all of its three names that is because as time goes shuttling back definitions become ever more difficult.

When Magda was just ten, Patrick Leigh Fermor passed through the city in his friend István's car with another friend, Angéla, beside him. Magda might have seen them as, having "stormed and bucketed" through Transylvania, they arrived at her home town, a place that was "not as perilous as it would have been in the winter season, with its parties and theatres and the opera in full blast" and where visitors could drink themselves silly at the New York in the main square, where the barman was supposed to have invented an undescribed but "amazing cocktail". It was a civilised, intoxicating sort of place, its history tangible in the cracked marble of the hotels and their vast grey mirrors even in 1993, when the city was in danger of starving and rotting away.

Now it is 1940. Nothing dreadful has happened yet and, as far as Magda's mother and father can tell, perhaps nothing will. It's just that the atmosphere is stifling. Year by year the beautiful city has grown more hostile. Magda has recovered from her rheumatic fever and is out and about again, though not in school. Some friends have organised a dance and brother Dezső is touting tickets near the station. Some of the Hungarian military labourers who have been doing work on the rail tracks – so this must be September at the earliest, after the Second Vienna Award – stop to buy a ticket, among them my father, László. Northern Transylvania is suddenly Hungarian again. He is Hungarian, albeit Jewish. Magda and Dezső are ethnically Hungarian, albeit Jewish. As Hungarians they are delighted to have become citizens of the same country so it's an occasion for rejoicing and no less so for Hungarian Jews. As a schoolboy László too had learned to chant *"Csonka magyarország nem ország. Egész magyarország mennyország"* – "Hungary cut is a land that's riven. Hungary whole is our true heaven" – like all the rest. He too is a patriot. Since this is only a partial restoration of the pre-war kingdom, it isn't quite heaven but a taste of heaven at least.

For László it is a break from labour, for Magda a chance to have some fun. László is just twenty-three, Magda sixteen. He goes to the dance and dances with a number of partners. It is all very decorous. The occasion might have been organised by a Jewish youth club, which is why Dezső is selling tickets, but it might be just an ordinary dance.

László and Magda dance together.

Then he goes back to work and she to her house and they don't meet again until she knocks at his door in Budapest with a cardboard box of negatives.

They discuss this possibility much later, once she is in the city. Maybe after her return from Penig. Maybe only once they are married, but the possibility is discussed. He remembers going to a dance, she recalls dancing with a man much like him. They were in the same place at the same time. Were they not? Why not?

Later, when I am recording him, László tells me this and I wonder whether she too has told me. I cannot quite remember. Nothing is fixed, nothing certain. Next time he tells me it is 1943, not 1940. She is home on a visit, he is working on the rail tracks, the story is essentially the same, but now it's December and he too has been home on leave and is back digging again. She is nineteen now and he is twenty-six. She has already been in Budapest for two years or more, has completed her apprenticeship with Escher and is making her own way as a photographer, or trying to. They are both swimming about in the grey pool of time until, at one point, they touch then part. Then in 1944 she arrives with the negatives and they meet, as for the first time.

What was it she saw in him? He has great dark eyes, a head of dark hair, is well proportioned, of slightly less than average height, and certainly fit because of all the work he has been doing, the kayaks he has been paddling and the mountains he has been hiking in. He was, she must have supposed, handsome enough but for that great hooked nose which was, nevertheless, somehow of a piece with him. She will have met many others more attractive or dashing. They would certainly have courted and propositioned her. She will have dated them and rejected them for a variety of reasons. Perhaps they were too forward. She might not have liked their hands or a look in their eyes. She might simply have been frightened of them. But now here is this man in uniform, in his family apartment, talking to her in that dark-brown voice, no doubt polite and, in his own manner, persuasive enough so they go down the stairs together and look forward to meeting again.

Is it calm she perceives in him, a calm harbour for her own wild inwardness? Does he smell of security, of a basic decency she has not found in others? Of beauty she might have seen enough. Her own brother was beautiful but distant, and preoccupied with passions that excluded her. Beauty had a cruel face.

22

The tide is sweeping her away from me. She is still at home in Cluj or Kolozsvár, also known as Klausenburg. She has left school and is studying photography wherever photography might then be studied. I have no image of her from that period so must guess at some composite of earlier and later photographs. Her obsessive presentation of herself and her children must have its roots here, most likely in her own mother who dressed her children in matching outfits. Magda, I suspect, won't ever have been a fully childish child. She seems to carry herself in a more adult way. The bouts of sickness probably played a part in that. She had tonsillitis at nine and it developed into rheumatic fever. The damp house they lived in might have been to blame, so they moved to another house overlooking the park, but it was no better. There was fungus in the hall, the rheumatic fever returned, and she was ill for a year. This is the year she told me about, when she stood at the window and waved to her friends in the park. It is winter yet also summer.

Snow falls
on the branches and a surface of sheer ice
where a mob of skaters wheel and weave petals

frilled with crystals. Transylvanian lace.
My mother's home town. The trees are thick with green.
Summer. Somewhere, in another place,

the skaters move to a frozen music between
the trees, performing a slow dance along the brink
of a precipice that cannot be seen

from where they are. They are lines of ink
impossible to read now. A fountain jets
snow. The bandstand is a skating rink

full of toy soldiers. Above them the sun sets
and rises and sets again. My mother leans
on her elbows. Her brother pirouettes

across the lake. She is ill. A tree screens
the hidden steps which lead up to a hot
clear patch of sunlight. The ice queen

melts in a derelict house. A flowerpot
dangles dry stems in the park. Where are we?
The skaters move in the distance, shot

through with dead light. Their translucency,
their quick black feet remind me of birds.
The house says nothing, staring vacantly

into the bushes. Above it vague herds
of clouds meander . . .

It was summer when we were there. It was hot in the street beside the park. The pond was not a lake and seemed barely big enough to accommodate a mob of skaters. We kept flicking between what she had described and what we actually saw. It was another place, impossible to know, but there she is leaning on one elbow. She watches her brother skating amongst her friends. The skaters leave lines behind them as if they are writing. It is all happening at once.

To her this is a single event, possibly a combination of other similar events. Maybe it's the wrong park. Maybe she has combined all the skaters of a year into one single vignette full of skating, waving and sickness. She is on one side of life, they on another. Her friendships were always intense and intimate, but now she is abandoned. They don't visit her as much as she would want. They let her down. It's what people do so you have to grab them and hold them ever closer, to not let them escape.

23

László told me the following story.

"Erzsébet met her husband to be, Sándor Nussbächer, at a dance in a club in Cluj or Kolozsvár, also known as Klausenburg, where he was working in a factory as a technician. The factory produced chocolates and candies. He left the company which was going bust and began to work for a big wine and spirit merchant. That was about 1920. So when Magda was born in 1924 he was a representative for this wine company. They lived quite a comfortable life and her mother never worked as such. They were a petit-bourgeois family. They had a maid as was usual and one of the grandmothers was staying with them. They also had a small house in Zilah as Hungarians know it, Zalau to Romanians, a small town without blocks of flats. But her father lost his job in 1929 as a result of the Crash and went to America for two years to try his luck. He sent home small amounts of cash. It was a great pity we never met."

The father's name was Sándor or Samuel or Samu. I'll call him Samuel for convenience. He was the son of Lipót and Zseni Nuszbacher (another spelling), Lipót being described in one document as a tailor, in another as a teacher, and in the third as a teacher of religion. Samuel was born in Cluj or Kolozsvár, also known as Klausenburg, in 1888, the third of three children following Nathan, born in 1884, and a sister Rezi, born 1886, who died in infancy. The family lived in the city centre. But Samuel must have spent time in Zilah and met his wife Erzsébet in that period, so the location of their meeting at the dance, as László gave it, seems unlikely since Magda herself was born in Zilah, in 1924. They probably moved back to Cluj or Kolozsvár, also known as Klausenburg, shortly after. He may well have worked in the chocolate factory, then at the wine merchant's there, but he was certainly absent for a while before returning on at least one occasion because, some years later, a man with his name appears on the Jewish Council.

Samuel wasn't around for long since, four years after Magda's birth, on February 23, 1928, he, as Samuel, is registered as a stowaway on the S.S. *Patagonia* in New York, having made the crossing from Antwerp, and sent to Ellis Island along with a certain Emanuel Mendel, another Jew from Transylvania. That there were only two stowaways on board, and that they came from the same original place, suggests a plan, but why was that necessary in 1928, before the Crash? And what happened then?

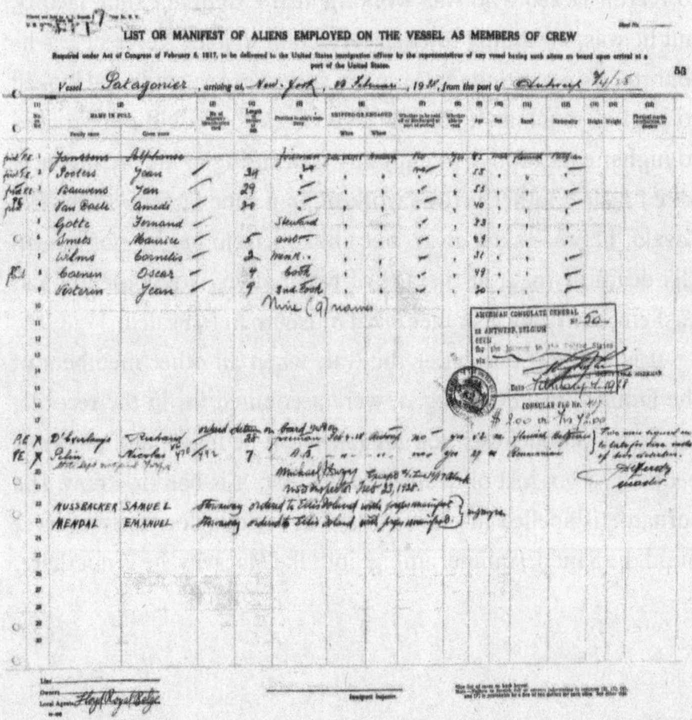

LIST OR MANIFEST OF ALIENS EMPLOYED ON THE VESSEL AS MEMBERS OF CREW

Required under Act of Congress of February 5, 1917, to be delivered to the United States immigration officer by the representatives of any vessel having such aliens on board upon arrival at a port of the United States.

58

Vessel Patagonier, arriving at New York, 19.., from the port of Antwerp

No. on List	Family name	Given name	Length of service	Position in ship's company	Age
1	~~Janssens~~	~~Alphonse~~		~~fireman~~	
2	Peeters	Jean	34		58
3	Bauwens	Jan	29		55
4	Van Baele	Amedé	30		40
5	Gotte	Fernand		Steward	23
6	Smets	Maurice	5		
7	Wilms	Cornelis	2		31
8	Coenen	Oscar	4	Cook	49
9	Vesterin	Jean	9	2nd Cook	30

Nine (9) names

AMERICAN CONSULATE GENERAL No. 50
at ANTWERP, BELGIUM
SEEN
for the journey to the United States
Date February 4, 1928
CONSULAR FEE No.

$ 2.00

AUSSBACKER SAMUEL Stowaway ordered to Ellis Island with proper manifest

MENDAL EMANUEL Stowaway ordered to Ellis Island with proper manifest

Feb 23, 1928.

Lloyd Royal Belge

Erzsébet was twelve years younger, born to David Kardos and Berta Mankowitz. She had a sister and two brothers. All were killed in the Holocaust except cousin Feri, the one relative we found in old age, who first showed us round Cluj or Kolozsvár, also known as Klausenburg, in 1993.

Dezső, Magda's beautiful older brother, also died. It is not known exactly when or where, but he is remembered in a book by Egon Balas who was to become a prominent applied mathematician in America with a string of prizes but who, like all Jews in Hungary at that time (and Northern Transylvania had been again under Hungarian control since 1940), was doing lowly manual work in the city. Balas joined the secret Communist Party and tried to recruit Dezső who was working at the Dermata shoe factory, but he was, according to Balas, reluctant to join. Nevertheless he reported on conditions at Dermata, spread propaganda and looked to help as much as he could. Like László he would not proceed to higher education or occupy any post fitting to his intelligence. Like László's father he was working in a shoe factory. Then, like László, he was taken away, but unlike László he did not return. His death in 1944, at the age of twenty-two, is recorded at Yad Vashem, the Holocaust memorial museum in Jerusalem.

It is striking that, after the war, when all other members of the family, including Magda, were accounted for in the records, her father Samuel was not. Mistakes can be made, and plenty of people just got lost or decided to get lost. It is hard to know. His surname is spelled in various ways in various documents, never mind the Sándor/Samuel ambiguity. Like Macavity, he is not there.

24

It is not impossible that he deserted the family and did not send money home. How could he have from Ellis Island? That may have been an invention of Erzsébet's, something to tell the children, but Magda never admitted to it. Erzsébet might or might not have known about stowing away and the arrest, but she would certainly know he was gone, with a clear idea as to why. According to one set of 1944 records he seems to have returned from America because a person with the same name appears on the list of Jews in the city, but then he vanishes again. His name, unlike his son's, is not recorded at Yad Vashem. He wouldn't have been the first or last to disappear – a great many did – but having once managed to stow away he might have done so again.

Both father and brother made a mark on Magda, but she was away in Budapest when everyone vanished.

That was shortly after March 19, 1944, just as László and Magda were enjoying a brief meeting over a coffee in Budapest. That was the day they saw the Germans arrive and knew the world had suddenly changed and darkened. But they did not know about Cluj or Kolozsvár, also known as Klausenburg. There the Jews were assured of safety at first but nine days later some hundred or more were rounded up. The Nazis quickly began seizing property. The young of the Halutz and Zionist movement were ready with forged documents that they could circulate amongst the community. Those who could escape tried to do so, either to Budapest or to Romania. Then the deportations began. Some of the young were, as László had been, pressed into the Hungarian Forced Labour Service and sent to support the front or else perform heavy labour with minimal food. The older ones tended to die but some of the fitter young men survived, though that too was owing more to luck than strength. Dezső would have been young and strong but he did not survive. Magda's story – and belief – was that he had died fighting as a partisan, but that was probably an illusion. Events moved fast. Within fifteen days from May 25 to June 9, 1944, more than 16,000 Jews were deported from Cluj or Kolozsvár, also known as Klausenburg, the majority to Auschwitz, Erzsébet among them. She was forty-four.

Magda did not know that. By this time she was living and working as best she could in Budapest. Her apprentice papers show her working for four employers in quick succession from October 1942 to February 1944. Only two of those employers appear in the trade directory of the time, one is a printer, the other a photographer. She spent three months with each but less than a month with the last. It was hard for Jews to keep their positions.

The apprentice sheet says nothing about Károly Escher and it begins when she is eighteen. Maybe the whole story of her being only sixteen is false, but it need not be. The document is a copy of an earlier one. Whoever completed it has written at the top that she had married since and was now László Szirtesné, her official married name, and had been since February 2, 1946.

25

Dezső might have been dead, but he had played an important and painful part in Magda's life. It must have been important because she told the story more than once. In it Dezső is asked to kiss his little sister but refuses, and when he is forced to do so he is violently sick. She does not say how old he was at the time or what affection developed between them afterwards. She clearly adored him, perhaps all the more for his first vehement rejection. It may be that her father was absent more often, for longer periods than she ever told us. For why, after all, would she have told us? Why would she have described his broad hat, his relaxed, confident smile, the timbre of his voice? She never described her mother, Erzsébet, never passed any memory of her on to us. It may be that her mother, like her brother, was all too important to her. Maybe the rejection by her brother seemed a core part of love, something that drove her own fierce affections and demands for continual, intense assurance. Dezső might also have represented some ideal of masculinity: handsome, strong, intelligent, heroic, distant, one that she dreamed of and desired but did not seek. She hoped to get news of him at Ravensbrück and again at Penig, hopeless as that was. But giving up was not her style. Maybe the sight of people dying around her made her all the more obstinate.

There are ever more maybes and perhapses now. Perhaps that apparently stable bourgeois Jewish household was neither stable nor bourgeois. Maybe it was just bourgeois enough to make her unreliable from the party's point of view. Maybe she did dance with László back in Cluj or Kolozsvár, also known as Klausenburg, at the age of sixteen, or possibly seventeen. Maybe she came to Budapest as an eighteen-year-old with some qualifications and not unqualified at sixteen. Maybe her father had returned having managed to send money home in hard times. Maybe the decision to try his luck in America was taken in a calm, deliberate fashion, but it is just as possible, indeed more likely, that it was an act of desperation. Maybe it was desperation that led him to stow away on the S.S. *Patagonia*. Maybe he was a desperate man. But maybe he was simply a rogue. I quite like to think of him as a rogue, a picturesque rogue with a line of smooth talk who cuts an almost romantic figure. Why not have a romantic rogue? Why not have a missing rogue of a father?

Everyone betrays you. Everyone harms you. Even women, those guards in Ravensbrück and Penig, betray and harm you, but they don't reject you, not entirely, or at least there is a hope they might not reject you. Might they not share your own sense of rejection? You could dress your children as you yourself might have been dressed. They could, perhaps, be you, only happier.

A fog settles at this point and I can't see through it. Perhaps I don't even want to because it isn't information I am seeking: it is something I already know or suspect. It is the form of understanding that enables two bodies to call to each other without speaking, though all that remains of such a body in her case are five early family photographs that she brought with her from

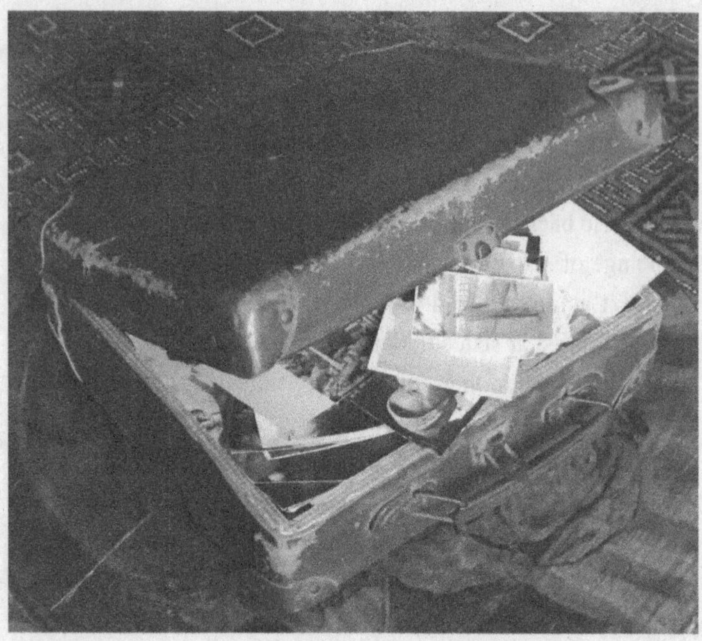

Cluj or Kolozsvár, also known as Klausenburg. It was I who carried them across the border along with other photographs of various periods, in a baby typewriter case I still have and keep under my desk.

THREE

Five Photographs

I am in a quandary now. I have taken her story as far as it can go: the rest can only be conjecture. I want to catch her, as if by surprise, in her early youth, but it is difficult since my most recent recollections of her are of the last years, of sickness, madness, and death. It is hard to forget the crashing of the ambulance after the overdose, the latest and last of the overdoses. It is almost impossible to put the end before the beginning.

What I would like to present to somebody – to her perhaps, or just to me – is the voice and energy, not of someone sick and dying but of a woman in her prime. I would like to bottle that prime as one might bottle a drink that could be poured into a glass and tasted exactly as once I tasted it.

The photographs I have are all studio photographs. There is nothing spontaneous about them. They are carefully posed for the purpose. But what is that purpose? Why are the people there, in that studio, at that time? Are the photographs taken there for sending to friends or relatives? Are they for sticking into an album at regular points in time so as to leave posterity with something presentable, like a calling card, professional, but a little flattering, not reality, but a proper picture one can show the world, one showing one's best side, in the best possible lighting, at the optimum moment, and beyond the moment? And what of the process that is to follow in the darkroom and over the light-box, the further flattery that involves retouching all the minor imperfections, a spot here, a stray hair there, the wrinkles on the neck, the bags and shadows under the eyes, and then, once that is done, more wonderful still, the tender colouring up of a pale cheek into a healthy pink, the slight reddening of the lips, the brightening of the eyes? The mummifying. The art. The pathos.

It's work. My work, she says from the telephone booth at the back of my mind. Don't sneer at it.

Her voice startles me. I am not sneering, I plead, but am not sure I am telling the truth. She has always had the knack of making me feel as though I were lying. Have you done your homework? Have you been drawing on your exercise book? Have you been careless again? Don't you realise how much depends on it?

The photograph is not dated. I gaze at her sixteen- or is it her fourteen-year-old face? Her shoulders are narrow and she is wearing a sailor collar. It may even be a school uniform. But the face is older, self-aware. It has, I am faintly disturbed to notice, a sexualised edge. It's there in the eyes, the adult eyes, in the way they look up at you, and in the faint ironic smile. She is beautiful and understands what that means. She is on the threshold of something I can only understand from my own life, my own most romantic period, in my mid-teens when all beauty seemed radiant, unattainable, faintly contemptuous, a gift that would not be offered, whose very purpose was denial. Did she know this, even then?

Of course I knew it, I hear her saying. But I didn't talk about it. Talking to you when you were fifteen was like talking to a wildly sensitive animal, all fur and shudder. Whenever I tried to touch you, you recoiled. I felt I repelled you. The more I wanted to comfort you the more repulsive I felt.

Being touched by you, I reply, was like being dragged back into your lap, like a child, like being unmanned while straining to be a man. You wouldn't understand, I say. I say it very quietly so she won't hear. But she'll know something is not right. She always does.

I accuse her of flirting. Surely those eyes are flirting! Your hair may be parted neatly and innocently in the middle, but you know what you are doing. You may even be wearing lipstick. What is that shine on your lips? Have you plucked your eyebrows? Those eyebrows are far too neat. At least your neck is not quite perfect. It is, in my judgment, a little short. You can't do much about that. Thank God you are not perfect.

I recognise the adult woman in her. Her early face is a premonition of her late face. As soon as I think that, her late face appears and stares at me. Her late eyes bore into me. They are the same as her early eyes, only more tired, more at the edge of exhaustion and desperation.

Right now she is babbling something. She is working up her anger. If you but knew, she is muttering. If you but knew a half, a quarter, a tenth, a hundredth of it. If you knew the chasm between the face in that photograph and the one you remember, this one, thirty years later! How old are you now? Seventeen years older than I was when I died. You know nothing. You are of no help to me.

And it is true. I know nothing and am of no help.

My eyes linger on the light stripes of her collar and on the bow that holds the collar together. What is that material? It looks winter- or autumn-weight, flat, featureless, almost starched. Its one single crease is heavy and slow. The stitching over the shoulder vanishes into it.

I am keeping my eyes off her face. I am fearful of recognising it too much. I prefer to think of the process out of which the image has emerged. I imagine the silence of the studio, the camera on its tripod, the light arranged, not too close to her face, shining through translucent paper so that it should be diffused and flattering. Did anyone retouch those features, did anyone give that hair a final brush? Was the sepia brown a way of softening her? And when the picture was done did she get off a chair or stool, stand up, shake her head to free her hair, pat down her dress, move her body and stretch her limbs so as to shrug the stiffness of posing out of her? What news of the war? Are her parents keeping their heads down, pretending not to be Jews in order not to be harassed? Where are they anyway? Presumably in the studio, keeping quiet. When she walks home do neighbours stop at their windows and think, There goes that pretty Jewish girl. Not one of us.

She has by then had her first brush with death. It was in the damp house where she contracted pneumonia and rheumatic fever at the age of fourteen. That was what kept her out of school for a year and damaged her heart for the rest of her life. The scene of her gazing out of the window while her friends are skating on the park pond has already happened. She might even have completed her first course in photography. She must know she wants to be a photographer and be thinking of an apprenticeship in the big, metropolitan city where everyone speaks her home language. But she cannot do that yet because the Second Vienna Award has not come into force so her city is still in Romania, not in Hungary. Hungary is a foreign country waiting to embrace her as one of its own.

I was never one of Hungary's own, she frowns. They soon let me know that.

We have moved out of the studio and are walking together down the street. The street is unfamiliar to me. It could be any street busy enough for a photographer's studio. There is more than one, as many as nine or ten. We pass them all.

I would take a better picture of myself, she says. It would make more sense to you. I wouldn't gaze at you like that. I wouldn't want to hurt you. I wouldn't even try to interest you. Then I could love you from a distance without being your mother. As she reaches out to take me by the arm I begin to pull away.

I catch a faint trace of perfume, but I cannot identify it.

If Magda was beautiful in youth, her brother, Dezső, was no less so. It is 1940 and I imagine the photographer, Weiss, my invented name for him, welcoming the seventeen-year-old Dezső into the studio. Dezső is so attractive I am tempted to make Weiss gay so that he might desire him as fiercely as my mother seemed to. When Dezső arrives, Weiss (not a handsome man in my imagination, but a short, fleshy Jew with a shiny moustache, a sort of Nazi caricature) greets him with genuine pleasure. He has not always done so in the past. Dezső had been moody and prickly as a boy, but now he has grown up. Perhaps he is less moody now, more reconciled to his sister. But she never forgets the rejection. It lies at the core of her version of him as the beautiful, sullen child retching at the touch of her. A few years later she has another version of him as the war hero dying in battle, or as a result of battle, actively, not passively, not at somebody else's behest, not wasted away to a skeleton and dumped in a mass grave as probably he was, but dying through some choice of his own, still sullen, still beautiful.

I don't know about beauty. It puzzles and dazzles me. I know it to be of the surface, but it can so penetrate the flesh that it seems to radiate from within. But what it radiates is hard to read and almost impossible to distinguish from the perfect, miraculous proportions that determine the outside. One searches the eyes for some warmth and that, one thinks, might be enough.

The words she herself used to signal visual pleasure were impersonal – "elegant", "tasteful", "charming" and *guszti* of course, but rarely "beautiful". She didn't talk about beauty much, not even when she settled down with my father to watch Miss World or Miss Universe on T.V. She was never daunted or made to feel inadequate or patronised by it. At least she never showed it. She sized up the contestants as a photographer might, objectively. Did they make a good picture?

It was different when she talked about Dezső, not in what she said about him but in the intensity with which she spoke. Or so I think now. Yet she stubbornly refuses to confirm my suggestion.

I imagine her eyes, her imagined eyes, full of tears. You are imagining again, she says. You keep inventing me. Inventing is lying. Are you lying to me?

There! Once again she has caught me in the act! Her long index finger points accusingly at me. Her nail varnish is a brilliant scarlet. It dazzles me. I turn my head away, back to him.

I examine him carefully. His hair is dense, dark and neat, his head well shaped, his ears elfin. His nose is perfectly proportioned, straight, neither snub nor hooked like my father's. (My father's people were never beautiful. He was a Jewish boy with big dark eyes and an enormous, unmissable nose, somewhat like mine.) Dezső's gaze resembles his sister's but is less flirtatious, more appraising, accusing, calm and steady, the eyes themselves not large but slender, leaf-shaped, one lid perhaps a touch lazy. His eyebrows are strong and clearly marked. His top lip is much thinner than his full bottom lip, the mouth not smiling but capable of smiling. His jaw is clear and masculine yet delicate, not pugnacious. His fine neck rises from an open collar and a warm tweed jacket. Now I am trying to see him together with Magda. They make a striking teenage pair walking down the street together.

I hated him at times, I hear her saying. I hated his moods, his aloofness, his brooding and self-importance. Her voice rises. She is about to shout. I turn her off, but the scent remains.

What perfume did she wear, I ask Clarissa. She thinks a little. She doesn't remember. It might have been Blue Grass, she says at last. Mid-range. She did not wear expensive perfume or expensive clothes. She might have given me a bottle. Very Sixties, she adds.

Weiss has retreated into his laboratory where the face of Dezső floats from the hypo tray into his hooded eyes: Dezső's troubled eyes, the pouting bottom lip, the clean-cut features.

Chubbier, less self-aware at the age of twelve or thirteen, in a folksy short-sleeved patterned dress complete with apron and a huge white Minnie Mouse bow in her hair, her head more adult than her body, she looks sweet but wrong, a china doll out of time and sequence. Her mother, it must be her mother, has dressed her as a winsome, innocent creature exquisitely located in the children's fashion of the time. If she is thirteen this must be 1937, the year

Disney released his first animated feature, *Snow White and the Seven Dwarves*. Surely she has been taken to see it! I look at her picture here and think of Snow White and all things Disney.

How she loved Disney! Disney was God, Father Christmas and the Fairy Godmother rolled into one. Our childhood pastel-coloured wardrobe was covered in transfers of the Seven Dwarves, each of whom she loved individually, Dopey, in his clumsiness, the best of all. I, like Dopey, was physically clumsy as a child, absent-minded, always tripping up, knocking things over. *Gabi mozdult!* George moved! they joked when something went tumbling back in Budapest. It became a catchphrase that stuck with me. Later, in England, she found a lanky cloth doll with long limbs, a Pinocchio nose and a green felt hat, his face lit by big, wide eyes and a mischievous but gormless grin. It looked nothing like me, but it stood in for me. I didn't want that image projected onto me. I felt gormless and helpless enough, thank you. Leaving home was leaving him.

My darling, Today we received your postcard. I can't describe the happyness. Please, please write as often as you can.

Is this picture of her an image of "happiness"? It would be good to think so. I see the same eyes as in the last photograph, but this time without the self-knowledge. Nothing dreadful has happened yet. The eyes are interested and a little wary but they do not imagine themselves. They are not objects. They don't yet know what they radiate, are merely on the threshold of that knowledge. Within three years her life will change. Within a year she will be so ill the rest of her life will be affected by it. Two years after that she will be in Budapest as a young apprentice photographer. Four more years and she will be in Ravensbrück.

Running the film forwards like this is like hanging a terrible weight above her childhood while knowing it can't be shifted.

What is to come is what is to come. She is about to dive into her life. It can't be helped, says the shrug of my inner survivor, the man who never did dive off the top board. My inner survivor's board was never high. He stepped cautiously into the water, tested the temperature then slipped in, spent some time there, then walked up the concrete steps back to the side of the pool.

One summer afternoon we were at the great open-air Széchenyi baths in Budapest when a boy stole the ball my brother and I were playing with, ran off and leapt into the pool with it. I ran after him into the water and went straight down until a stranger reached after me and plucked me out. I don't think I had ever before thought of water as dangerous, certainly not as deep or as shocking.

I don't know where this memory is leading me, perhaps to the prospect of death and thence back to the face in the photograph.

Now that I return to it I look closer and see the picture isn't all innocence and unknowing. The head is too big, the body too small. The prominent, almost goofy teeth she inherited from her mother seem to be pressing uncomfortably at the lips. One tooth is darker than the rest. As for the eyes, they are a little too open. There is fear in them. Their intense appraisal is beyond mere curiosity. Come to think of it, the teeth and the eyes give her an unhinged look. Her white Minnie Mouse bow becomes a strange growth billowing from her brain. The shawl collar and the apron turn to cream. She is covered in cream.

She does look a little crazy, doesn't she? I could write a caption under the picture, as in a medical study, reading: *Thirteen-year-old girl in the early stages of psychosis, Romania 1937*. The rose of her adult fury is budding in her, so I can sense the full-grown woman inside her, svelte, not quite steady, her face in shadow, her hand raised, ready to strike. The full flower of psychosis.

It would be an invention, of course, as is this whole book, this long caption to explain not only her psychosis but the psychosis of a world that was about to enter a war. But that would be a caption under a caption. The captions are infinite. Any face looks crazy when you look at it long enough, if you come across it when you yourself feel a little off-balance.

We've been waiting for what seemed ages for your letter. It made us very happy. I am very excited to hear everything. I am looking forward enormously to have you home.

It was as necessary for me to leave home as it was for her to be in constant touch. Write and keep writing. Let me know everything that happens even if nothing happens. Look after yourself. Remember your health, it's the most important thing, adds my father.

He probably meant her health. Looking after her was what he did. It was what his knowable, not his working life was about. She must not get too excited. Please don't upset her. Let's sit down and play rummy. Or whist.

But that was when she was, as we then understood, an invalid. She was not the striding, loud, combative, laughing, teasing siren she could be, the fervently generous woman who talked striptease and referred to pubic hair as Acker Bilk, the woman who danced in the snow and defied the party cadre's order that she report on others, the artist with the fine brush and the razor, the woman behind the lens.

Dear George,

Thank you very much for your letter and the consideration with wich you regard us. I know that you haven't much to say to me but I thought you'll have enough decency at least not to show.

You take love for mania, she says. You take love for possessiveness. You take love for clinging. You take love but don't give it. She doesn't say this to me, of course. Nor would I have dared bring her to the point when she might actually say it, or throw it all back at her, reverse the terms and say, you take mania for love, possessiveness for love, clinging for love. It is not because I wouldn't mean it but because it wouldn't be true. It would be palpably false.

Must life be so intense, so melodramatic?

She is shouting down the phone at me. I listen to her for as long as I can, then put the phone down. Who is this doll with the ridiculous bow? She could be anybody.

No. It could only be her.

It is 1928. I imagine her introducing me to her mother. Before me stands a fashionable middle-class woman with a heavy plaid jacket over a chemise. She is lovely, isn't she? says my mother. Not as lovely as you, I think, though I can see her in you. She has a bob like yours but her face is wider, her teeth a little more prominent, nevertheless she is you alright, those eyes and lips are immediately recognisable.

Pleased to meet you, Nussbächerné / Mrs Nussbächer. Do sit down. It was, I think, a family group you wanted, you with the two children, young Dezső and little Magda. Such lovely children, Nussbächerné. Now what shall we do with you? Let me think about the composition a moment, says Weiss, since it is his voice I am adopting.

He thinks about it. The mother, he knows, must be in the middle and the two children on either side. She could sit and they stand, or the children could sit together on the small bench and she lean over them. But that's too cramped. The answer might be to have the children on the bench with the mother standing behind them so they come up roughly to her chin. That is how I would do it. That is how Weiss does it.

Weiss adds subdued lighting to soften their features and give them contour, positioning Dezső furthest from the light so the left side of his face emerges from shadow and his dark-coloured shirt forms a nice bass note. That leaves Magda on the left. Should they smile? It is not good to force people to smile, it looks unnatural, best simply to ask them to look at the camera and, in the case of children, to give them something to look at. Weiss and I are in agreement on this.

So what should they look at?

Erzsébet Nussbächer (do I dare call her just by her first name, Erzsébet?) looks directly at the photographer, her mouth half open. Dezső glares into the space over the photographer's right shoulder at the shelf where the wind-up drummer monkey sits drumming, and Magda is gazing, wide-eyed, possibly at the monkey or at something else just above the monkey's hat. Her mouth is open, lost in wonder, a little startled perhaps, but so genuinely animated it doesn't look as though she is posing at all. Weiss and I see it from a photographer's point of view as three pairs of eyes, all with different expressions, all looking at something different. I like this picture. I like what the eyes are doing. We both do. I like Weiss. His life has a good sixteen years to run. I hope he uses them well.

As for me, I keep looking at the two children's faces because they make a pair and neither can be entirely detached from the other. The mother, Erzsébet Kardos, as she was born, is a mystery to me. All she is is what I see of her and what I recall of my own mother's minimal and fragmentary descriptions. She looks fun: the daughter of a large, respectable, middle-class Jewish family that no longer exists, a woman who married a handsome entrepreneurial man who was also fun, a bit of a chancer and charmer, a man who glittered in his brief appearances then vanished and returned to glitter before vanishing again. It's easy to conjure him out of almost nothing: nothing is easier. Snap your fingers and he appears. Or disappears, like his wife, my murdered grandmother.

But the children are so intensely present they do not disappear. I love Dezső's younger face, his determined frown, his solemnity, his disdainful clean-cut, child-Rimbaud look. I have always thought it the proper way to face the world. There is poetry behind the face. It forgives nothing and is as absolute as I imagine the seven-year-old Rimbaud's to have been.

Tout le jour il suait d'obéissance ; très
Intelligent ; pourtant des tics noirs, quelques traits,
Semblaient prouver en lui d'âcres hypocrisies.
Dans l'ombre des couloirs aux tentures moisies,
En passant il tirait la langue, les deux poings
À l'aine, et dans ses yeux fermés voyait des points

As Oliver Bernard has it in the English prose version I first read as a schoolboy:

> All day long he sweated with obedience; very intelligent; and yet certain unpleasant habits, characteristics, seemed to betray bitter hypocrisies in him! Passing along in the darkness of corridors with mildewed paper, he would stick out his tongue, his two fists in his groin; and he would see specks on his closed eyelids

That is how I wanted to imagine myself at seventeen, willing myself into the seven-year-old Rimbaud as he "obstinately shuts himself up in the coolness of the latrines", where "he would think in peace, surrendering his nostrils".

The Dezső-Rimbaud boy was the poetic condition as I first felt it, ever since I read Rimbaud at school, not in lessons, but in the small council flat in Burnt Oak where my fellow closet poet Stephen lived and where we would read to each other along with Ashley, also a closet poet but much more Rimbaudesque than I could be at the time. We were three struggling A-Level science students, staying up late to learn about the magic art of poetry, the hidden life that was also the true life of the world, then going home at two or three in the morning, drunk on it, in a condition almost as dangerous as if we had been really drunk.

This Dezső, this Rimbaud figure, who was physically sick when Magda kissed him, had somehow compressed into his own seven-year-old face the qualities that make and keep a poem glowing. Note, I want to add, the crease in the paper, the cracked white line that runs across his face like lightning, like a perfect symbol. This may be, I venture to myself, the way the young Magda regarded her brother, why she seemed to be so passionately in love with him despite being rejected by him. Having experimented with the thought, I leave him glowering at one side of the picture and return to Magda, my Little-Lord-Fauntleroy-collared, wonder-struck mother.

Where have I seen her expression before? Have I ever seen it? Could it have been her expression when she first saw the sea? When she stepped off the plane in England for the first time? Maybe earlier, when she first came to Budapest, the grand metropolis where her dreams of becoming a photographer, possibly a great photographer, might be realised? It is certainly a first something. I have a photograph my father must have taken of her standing by the window of our Budapest flat in her underwear, prized and self-possessed, prized and safe. But her expression isn't like this, not with this element of surprise and awe, or what I read as awe.

Back in the photograph Magda's mother returns the gaze of the photographer, her brother is lost in himself, and she is elsewhere, wherever her startled wide-open eyes are directed, which is not at my invented drummer monkey but at something else that she is seeing for the first time. Maybe you have to be a child to be as startled by the world, a young child at that, a child seeing a giraffe for the first time, or a puffin, or a penguin, or a clown or a conjuring trick. I can't find quite the same expression in any of her photographs of me, though there is one where I am staring into the window of a tiny toyshop and you don't see my face because she is behind me and I am only a very small person in a coat and a big cap.

Her eyes are vulnerable, of course. To be so lost in something is to be off your guard and therefore not quite safe. This is a child in need of protection. It is odd to think of her like that since nothing in her adult life suggested she needed protecting, not even in sickness. She would not have sheltered behind my father in a fight: she would have stood in front of him. She would certainly have stood in front of me. The truth is that she was, if anything, over-protective of her children and I rejected her protection. Protection implies weakness.

But her childhood gaze goes beyond vulnerability. There is, I am beginning to think, something mystical about it, as if she were rapt by a vision, a miracle beyond the conjurer's art. Maybe she has been vouchsafed a vision of her own incomprehensible future. I know photographs are still, but time tumbles about them chaotically, future and past indistinguishable, simultaneous, like voices in a storm. The storm seems to freeze for a moment but will not settle and starts up again.

There is another detail beyond the facial expression that I cannot help but notice; although I did miss it in the earlier picture. It is her earring (presumably the other of the pair is lost in shadow). It isn't a clip but a piercing. It startled my anglicised eyes the first time and still does, as though it should not be there, though the practice was common enough with girl children, both Catholics and Jews, the piercing being administered soon after birth. Later, in Magda's youth, the earring became part of her romance with gypsy life, a fantasy item, the earrings bigger, more conspicuous, a vital element in her attempts to look the part.

It is a nice coincidence that when Roland Barthes speaks of

the tiny incidental detail that moves him in a photograph he calls it a *punctum*, an "accident that pricks or bruises me". I can't distance myself sufficiently to discuss her in theoretical terms, but I look at her and know the earring pierces and fixes. It pins her to the card the photograph is printed on. It prevents her floating away and escaping. It pricks me. She is who she has to be, there and nowhere else.

About the same time as the triple portrait was taken, Magda's father, Sándor (or Samuel) Nussbächer was being photographed in another studio, not in Cluj but in Antwerp. It is a significant photograph in that very soon after it was taken, on February 23, 1928, as we already know, together with a man called Emanuel Mendel, he stowed away on the S.S. *Patagonia* bound for New York. This, in other words, is the photograph of a man about to commit a criminal act.

He looks respectable enough. Well dressed – indeed elegantly dressed – in a light-coloured homburg, with matching suit, waistcoat and a neat tie, he doesn't look as though he needs to stow away. He would feel perfectly at home, surely, strolling about on the deck of a liner as by right. There must have been money once, enough for that suit, and not too long ago, because it is an excellent fit for the heavily built man. Something must have gone wrong.

Maybe he was unlucky. But maybe he was not as respectable as he looks. There is something of Al Capone in his handsome self-assurance. He is a man used to giving orders of some kind. The generous lips are sensual, prepared to kiss. The nose is strong, a powerful feature ready to hand on to his descendants. One eye is cold, the other alert and it gives him the air of someone young and mature at the same time.

Not all of him is there in the sense that the photograph has been artfully faded at the edges so he appears to float out of a haunted wall, only his head and shoulders materialising, as if the rest of him were of less importance. I wonder if she ever saw him like that, with that looming presence, that expression as he entered his home and stood in the door or as he was leaving, towering over her, bending down to kiss her with those lips. That is precisely how he might have left, in that suit, with that hat, heading off into the February cold, wearing a coat and scarf, handsome devil, gambler, confidence man, chancer, vanishing act.

I can see him in both me and in my brother. If I turn away then glance quickly back, I think it is Andrew, but when I catch only his eye I think it's me. So that is what she did. It is him she gave birth to but in two parts, Andrew and me, then she put the two parts together to make a single one of him.

She was unlucky with the two men in her childhood, with the brother who rejected her and the father who deserted her then returned, only to vanish again without trace. She hung on to the photograph though, the only one of him, just as she hung on to the triple portrait including her mother. Was she any luckier with her sons?

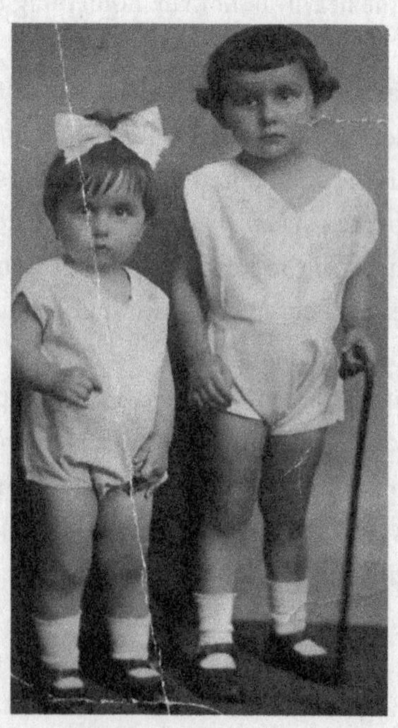

The earliest of the photographs shows Magda and Dezső at two and four respectively. Their outfits are identical: short, sleeveless white rompers, white socks and sandals (I too wore just such white socks and sandals). The two of them are standing next to each other on a carpet against a pale studio wall. Here too Magda wears a big white bow in her hair that has been arranged into a fringe with the bow – more ragged than the one in the later picture producing a tiny topknot, like a sprig of grass. Dezső has been given a child-sized walking stick as prop and holds it loosely but dutifully in his left hand, the other arm hanging tentatively at his side. He is not about to go walking. His hair is longer, flicked out at the side like Christopher Robin's and his expression is infinitely sad as if he had been terminally hurt in some way. Magda's expression is more challenging and enquiring. She is staring at the apparatus she herself will be using in the years to come. What is it? What does it do? Where am I? What is this about?

Little by little faces are stripped away, each revealing a new past and a new potential. How awkward she is here, barely standing, her left hand grasping at the bottom of her romper, the other formed into a loose fist at the end of her bent right arm. Her legs are sturdy enough so she won't be toppling forward or back. She is safe for now, angelic in white, a film still running forwards.

A long way forwards.

A few excerpts from her letters to me in Leeds.

I have baked a cake wich I hope won't be too stale at arrival. You know I can't bake, but I tried my best, to be able to send you a cake like a real mum.

I miss you first of all for yourself though you haven't been home a lot, but now you are not here is a great gap. Everything seems so still . . .

I hope the parcel has arrived all right and the cake was still palatable, didn't go off in the packet . . .

I enclose some prints. I've sent them back twice but still no good. If it would be up to me I would send them with the originals to Dixon headquarters . . .

I had a very bad week last week but now I feel much better. The old engine gave me a lot of trouble though I hardly did any work

Stray scraps of conversation but a voice at least, not the mad, exhausted voice on the birthday tape, but one as written, surprisingly well, with the odd slip in spelling. I am ridiculously pleased by her use of "palatable". I approve and pat her on the back. I give her a kiss.

For some reason I remember Hamlet's advice to the Players: Do not saw the air too much with your hand. Do not tear a passion to tatters. Suit the action to the word. Hold the mirror up to nature.

Take a deep breath. Calm yourself. Go on calculating.

THE DIVER

Hecht's diver magically returns to the high platform from which he has leapt. The board has stopped vibrating with his weight and is quite still. The water has healed, he is no longer in it, the hole has closed. It is as if the dive had never happened, and it hasn't.

Now my mother has almost risen to the top board. I have wound the film back there but only through a conjuring trick. (Conjure me, she seemed to say.) At one point I carried her across from the sick bay at Penig to a clean hospital bed, opened the window for her (thank you, she says), brought in some flowers (thank you), carried a tray of food to her (thank you), and sat beside her watching her recover so she could be wooed and dressed by my namesake, American George.

I would have liked to have done that for her in life, but I wasn't there, nor could have been. Later, when she was sick again, sick unto death, I could have been there but wasn't, so when people came and told me of her death I didn't know what to feel, or if I felt anything at all.

I don't have a photograph of my mother as a new-born child so I can't position her first appearance in life on the very top of the diving board. In fact I have no more photographs. I don't even have a recollection of her kissing me. Once, when Clarissa had encephalitis and ran a high fever, she dreamed that my mother kissed her, but she didn't kiss her in life. Some people just don't. As a small child I had been, as she herself wrote, her little squirrel, her one consolation. But that was then.

ACKNOWLEDGMENTS

Major thanks are due to Jeremy Cameron who first pressed me to write this book, gave me a time limit and a page length, then read it at its various stages; to Ringo Gründel in Germany who wrote to me out of the blue asking me to confirm that a name on the list of female prisoners arriving at Penig concentration camp was in fact my mother (it was) and who then invited me to Penig and helped enormously through his own researches and archives, as well as to his fellow researchers Janine, Uli, Tobi and Jan; to Dutch writer and friend Daan Heerma van Voss who read through the book in progress while I was in China and whose advice has been invaluable, and to Dai Fan whose invitation to a month-long residency in China gave me the time to concentrate on it. Just as important, in Hungary, were László Kúnos and dear Gabi Fekete (who passed away far too soon in 2018) who both always encouraged me in everything and were among the first to read the finished book.

Above all, belatedly, my thanks are due to my father, László Szirtes, to whom I talked on tape for more than two years after Magda's death and whose presence in a book in which he plays a supporting role, is vital. Though he died in 2010, he, like all good heroic people, really deserves to be the central character in his own story.

My constant thanks to my family: to my wife Clarissa, whose own knowledge of Magda complemented mine, to our children Tom and Helen, as also to my brother Andrew who helped build my picture of Magda; to Keiron Pim who advised me on research, as well as to Bill Swainson, to my agent Anna Webber who believed in the book and helped to shape it, and to Katharina Bielenberg whose advice and editing has been of enormous help.

And if American George is still alive and comes across this book and reads it, let him too be thanked for falling in love with Magda on her release from Penig and for supplying her with clothes and human warmth.

GEORGE SZIRTES was born in Hungary in 1948. He published his first book of poems, *The Slant Door*, in 1979. It won the Geoffrey Faber Memorial Prize. Among his many other poetry collections, *Reel* was awarded the T. S. Eliot Prize, for which he has twice been shortlisted since. He has in addition won various international prizes for poetry and for his translations of Hungarian poetry and fiction, including the Man Booker International Prize for his translations of László Krasznahorkai.

Since publication in 2019, *The Photographer at Sixteen* has been shortlisted for the PEN Ackerley Prize, the Jewish Wingate Prize, the Slightly Foxed Best First Biography Prize, and was the winner of the East Anglian Book Award (Biography and Memoir) and the James Tait Black Memorial Prize.